THE ECONOMICS OF CHILD CARE

THE ECONOMICS
OF CHILD CARE

EDITED BY

David M. Blau

RUSSELL SAGE FOUNDATION   NEW YORK

The Russell Sage Foundation

The Russell Sage Foundation, one of the oldest of America's general purpose foundations, was established in 1907 by Mrs. Margaret Olivia Sage for "the improvement of social and living conditions in the United States." The foundation seeks to fulfill this mandate by fostering the development and dissemination of knowledge about the political, social, and economic problems of America.

The Board of Trustees is responsible for oversight and the general policies of the Foundation, while administrative direction of the program and staff is vested in the President, assisted by the officers and staff. The President bears final responsibility for the decision to publish a manuscript as a Russell Sage Foundation book. In reaching a judgment on the competence, accuracy, and objectivity of each study, the President is advised by the staff and selected expert readers. The conclusions and interpretations in Russell Sage Foundation publications are those of the authors and not of the Foundation, its Trustees, or its staff. Publication by the Foundation, therefore, does not imply endorsement of the contents of the study.

Library of Congress Cataloging-in-Publication Data

The economics of child care / edited by David M. Blau.
    p. cm.
    Includes bibliographical references and index.
    ISBN 0-87154-118-1
    ISBN 0-87154-119-X (pbk)
    1. Child care services—Economic aspects—United States.
    I. Blau, David (David M.)
    HQ778.7.U6E26   1991   91-17321
    649'.1—dc20   CIP

First Papercover Edition 1995

RUSSELL SAGE FOUNDATION
112 East 64th Street, New York, NY 10021

10 9 8 7 6 5 4 3 2 1

To Janet, Kathryn, and Michael

Contents

About the Authors

David Blau is associate professor of economics and fellow of the Carolina Population Center at the University of North Carolina at Chapel Hill. He has devoted considerable time and effort to studying economic aspects of child care in the past five years, and together with Philip Robins is the author of one of the first studies to document the effect of child care costs on the labor force participation rate of women. He is also coeditor of a special issue of the *Journal of Human Resources* on child care.

Rachel Connelly is assistant professor of economics at Bowdoin College, and recently completed a one-year Census Research Fellowship at the Census Bureau. She has published articles on the impact of cohort size on earnings and on occupational choice under uncertainty. Professor Connelly has authored several papers on economic aspects of child care and has been an active participant in the public policy debate on child care, appearing as a panelist at the Family Impact Seminar on Capitol Hill in a session on the market for child care.

Sandra Hofferth is senior research associate at the Urban Institute, where she is currently project director of the National Child Care Survey and co-principal investigator of the Profile of Child Care Settings Study. Dr. Hofferth has published widely on child care and related issues such as family structure, children's living arrangements, and adolescent pregnancy and childbearing. She testified before two Congressional Committees in 1989 on her child care research.

Ellen Eliason Kisker is a researcher at Mathematica Policy Research, Inc. (MPR), where she has done extensive research on child care issues. She is currently directing the Profile of Child Care Settings Study for the U.S. Department of Education. Dr. Kisker has been integrally involved in the design and conduct of a study of before-and-after school programs and is a member of the advisory panel for a national study of child care demand for the U.S. Department of Health and Human Services. As a senior researcher for the Teenage Parent Demonstration Evaluation, Dr. Kisker has also conducted a study of the child care markets in the areas served by the demonstration and assessed the early impacts of this mandatory work/welfare program on child care choices and use.

Rebecca Maynard is vice president of Mathematica Policy Research, Inc. (MPR). Dr. Maynard directs the research activities in MPR's Princeton office and specializes in research in welfare, employment, child care, and other social service policies. She is currently directing a major six-year demonstration sponsored by the U.S. Department of Health and Human Services to test alternative program models to promote self-sufficiency among welfare-dependent teenage parents and is working with the U.S. Department of Labor on the design of employer-sponsored child care initiatives. She served on the National Academy of Sciences Panel on Child Care Policy, is currently serving on an advisory committee for the President's Commission on Children, and recently directed a major survey of child care needs and options available in low-income areas.

Deborah Phillips is assistant professor of psychology at the University of Virginia and was recently a mid-career fellow at the Bush Center in Child Development and Social Policy at Yale University. Her recent research has focused on the effects of child care on children's social and emotional development and on the role of child care staff in influencing the quality of child care. She has written extensively on public policy issues in the area of child care and has testified numerous times before Congress.

William Prosser has worked in the Office of the Assistant Secretary for Planning and Evaluation, U.S. Department of Health and Human Services, since 1973. He has conducted research and developed legislation on issues such as child care, Head Start, foster care, teen pregnancy, and other family issues. In the mid-1970s he directed the Congressionally mandated study of the Appropriateness of Federal Interagency Day Care Regulations. More recently, he has been involved in designing evaluations of JOBS and Transition Benefits provisions of the Family Support Act of 1988.

Philip Robins is professor of economics and chairman of the economics department at the University of Miami and is a research affiliate of the Institute for Research on Poverty at the University of Wisconsin-Madison. He is an expert on the economics of public transfer programs and is currently studying child support enforcement policies. Professor Robins has been studying child care issues for more than fifteen years, and is currently conducting (with David Blau) a comprehensive study of the interrelationships among fertility, employment, and child care use.

James Walker is assistant professor of economics at the University of Wisconsin-Madison. He is also affiliated with the Institute for Research on Poverty and the Economics Research Center at NORC. His current research focuses on the effects of social programs on life cycle behavior, especially the decision making of women. In addition to his work on child care in the United states, Dr. Walker is engaged in a long-term project evaluating the effects of social programs in Sweden.

Acknowledgments

Most of the chapters in this volume are revisions of papers that were originally presented at the Carolina Public Policy Conference on "The Economics of Child Care" at the University of North Carolina at Chapel Hill on May 16, 1990. The conference and the preparation of the manuscript were supported by a grant from the Russell Sage Foundation. I am very grateful to the Foundation, and to Peter De Janosi, in particular, for the generous support that made this undertaking possible. I am also grateful to the editorial staff at the Russell Sage Foundation, particularly Lisa Nachtigall and Charlotte Shelby, for their assistance in preparing the manuscript. I thank Linda Waite for helpful comments on the manuscript. Finally, I thank Sarah Mason and Zelma Myers at the University of North Carolina for their considerable assistance in organizing the conference. Their help was indispensable in making the conference a success.

Introduction

David M. Blau

Child care has attracted an increasing amount of attention in recent years from a wide variety of groups. As mothers of young children have entered the labor force in dramatically large numbers over the past two decades, sociologists, child development experts, advocacy groups, and policymakers have placed child care high on the research and policy agenda. Sociologists and psychologists have studied the social, economic, and demographic forces driving increased numbers of mothers of young children into labor force participation, the consequences for families and society of the need to provide child care during the mother's working hours, and the consequences to children of alternative types of child care arrangements. Child care advocacy groups have succeeded in forming a broad coalition of organizations committed to achieving increased government support for and involvement in child care. It is argued that this is essential to prevent the supposed lack of accessible, affordable, high-quality child care in the United States from becoming a major impediment to the well-being of families with young children. Policymakers from across the political spectrum have responded with an enormous variety of new proposals, and the debate over child care policy has recently occupied a prominent place on the political agenda.

It is widely recognized that economic issues are an important part of the debate over child care policy. These issues include, but are not limited to, the responsiveness of child care demand

and supply to prices, the efficiency of the child care market, the economic rationale for government subsidies and regulation of child care, and the role of employers in providing child care. Until recently, very little research by economists had addressed these issues in a manner that could provide useful guidance to policymakers. There are now, however, a substantial number of economists engaged in serious scholarly research on crucial economic issues in child care. The need for such research is pressing if policymakers are to have a basis for well-informed decisions. And, importantly, the results of the research must be presented to as wide an audience as possible in order to make the debate over child care policy a rational one.

This volume presents results from state-of-the-art economic analyses of child care issues in a form accessible to the nonspecialist. The chapters have been written by economists who are engaged in path-breaking work on child care. The results of this research have to date typically been published in academic economics journals or in technical reports to sponsoring agencies. The authors of the chapters in this book have recognized the need to disseminate their findings to a wide audience and have consequently written papers that report their research results in a nontechnical way, but without sacrificing their key insights. The goal of the volume is to bring basic principles and findings of the economic analysis of child care into wide currency among groups and individuals with a strong interest in and knowledge of child care issues but without the expertise to conduct or evaluate sophisticated economic research. Economists with an interest in child care should also find the volume useful.

The authors herein address some of the most important issues that have arisen during recent policy and scholarly debates on child care. The economic perspective on these issues is often quite distinct from the perspective of other disciplines. The unique contribution of the economic perspective on these issues is to clarify some of the fundamental sources of disagreement in the debate over child care policy. In the following paragraphs I sketch some of these key issues and summarize the approaches to them developed in the book.

The first and, in some ways, most basic issue to which economists can contribute is the rationale for government involvement in child care. This issue was not prominent in the recent debate leading to the passage in 1990 of major new child care legislation. Apparently, there is widespread agreement on the need for government subsidization and regulation of child care.

The debate centered instead on the size and form of government intervention. But the fundamental question of why government involvement in child care is desirable at all is extremely important, and economics provides a natural framework in which to address it. As summarized in the paper by James Walker, there are two basic reasons that society might wish for government intervention in the market for child care services. The first is inefficiency: if there is some source of imperfection in the child care market that prevents it from operating so as to maximize consumer welfare, *and* if the government can itself avoid the problems that led to the imperfection, then government intervention to improve the functioning of the market is warranted. The second possible reason for government intervention is inequity: if the distribution of child care services generated by the market is considered inequitable to consumers, then intervention can be justified. Efficiency and equity issues are closely related and are both of profound concern to those who are involved in child care. Nevertheless, as discussed by Walker, separation of the issues clarifies the motivation for government intervention. Efficiency is the natural starting point for analysis, since understanding how the market operates logically precedes normative evaluation of how the resulting services should be distributed.

Philip Robins, James Walker, and Ellen Kisker and Rebecca Maynard all argue in their chapters that an important source of potential inefficiency in the child care market is that parents may be poorly informed about the quality of care their children are receiving. Subsidies may induce parents to purchase higher quality care; regulations may prevent low quality care from being offered by providers; and government-sponsored consumer education may improve parents' ability to discern quality in child care. Walker offers an important note of caution, however. Before government intervention can be justified on these grounds, it must be determined that the government is better able than parents to measure quality and enforce regulations governing quality. Walker argues that it is not at all obvious that this is the case. Kisker and Maynard propose that the government's advantage over consumers in this area is its ability to use information on quality generated in research by child development experts. This leads directly to the second main issue common to the papers in the volume: child care quality.

Because the quality of child care is of central importance to child care policy, it is discussed throughout the volume. Two important themes emerge from the discussion in the chapters. First, quality is a shorthand notion for a variety of attributes of child care. It is often analytically convenient to model child care services as if quality were unidimensional and each provider could be ranked on a single scale in terms of the quality offered. This approach is typically used in formal economic models of child care, as discussed in the paper by Philip Robins. The papers by James Walker and me emphasize that a child care arrangement consists of a bundle of attributes, such as group size, child–staff ratio, the nurturing given by the providers, the educational opportunities offered, convenience to the parents, reliability, and numerous others. This leads to important decisions that must be made by parents in weighing various attributes against one another and considering the specific needs of their child at a given age when choosing a provider. Second, the measure of child care quality developed by child development experts tends to put heavy weight on those attributes of arrangements that promote child development, as measured by standard instruments such as the Peabody Picture Vocabulary Test. Several of the chapters stress the fact that parents may care about other aspects of child care in addition to those considered by the child development field. Philip Robins and Rachel Connelly both argue that increased expenditure on child care by parents leads almost by definition to improved child care quality from the perspective of the parents. But there is no guarantee that increased expenditure, whether due to government subsidies or other causes, will lead to increased quality from the perspective of child development. Kisker and Maynard and I discuss evidence concerning the relationship between quality as defined in the child development literature and parental expenditure on child care, and conclude that there is little evidence of a positive association. Both chapters discuss the possible consequences of government subsidies that are tied to the use of providers meeting regulations intended to promote child development.

A third important issue that is discussed in several of the chapters is the behavior of consumers in the child care market. Economists have a well-developed set of tools for analyzing consumer behavior, and several of the chapters discuss in detail how these tools can be applied to study a particularly important issue, the response of consumers to increased government subsidies for child care expenses. Rachel Connelly presents convincing evidence that the labor force participation decisions of women are influenced by the cost of child care they face. Women who would have to pay a relatively high price for child care are, other things being equal, less likely to work. Philip Robins describes evidence indicating that parental expenditures on child care are sensitive to the price of child care. These observations imply that increased government child care subsidies to consumers will induce more women to join the labor force and will cause the average quality of purchased care, as viewed by parents, to increase. These are potentially important effects of increased government child care subsidies that should be considered when evaluating the likely consequences of such increases.

The final main issue of importance discussed in the volume is the supply of child care. If there are imperfections in the child care market, they are generally thought to occur on the supply side, so careful analysis of the supply of child care is a crucial component of a complete analysis of the rationale for government intervention. Some particularly vexing queries concerning the supply of child care services are why child care providers receive such low wages, experience high turnover, and receive little or no reward in the market for costly investments in education and specialized training. James Walker discusses these and related issues at length in his chapter. He summarizes evidence suggesting that the child care market is characterized by substantial heterogeneity of providers, particularly in the family day care sector. Unregulated providers appear in general to be disinterested in maximizing income from child care by advertising and investing in improved service quality. Entry and exit from the market are low-cost actions for providers of this type, leading to an effective ceiling on wages and little incentive to attempt to meet standards imposed on the regulated sector. Regulated providers behave more like "firms" attempting to maximize profits, but their relatively low earnings impose limits on their ability to invest in meeting tighter standards.

The issues discussed above by no means exhaust the areas in which economic analysis of child care can provide useful insights. Among the many other issues discussed in the chapters in this volume are the conditions under which the existence of waiting lists for slots in day care centers provides evidence of a shortage of child care; an analysis of the effects of regulation of child care inputs on the quality of child care provided; the relationship between the cost of child care and participation by low-income single mothers in the Aid to Families with Dependent Children (AFDC) program; and proposals designed to make the distribution of child care services more equitable. In the following paragraphs I summarize the contents of each of the chapters.

In "Child Care Policy and Research: An Economist's Perspective," Philip Robins presents a broad overview of child care trends and policies in the United States, and describes, both in general terms and with reference to examples from his own research, how economic analysis can illuminate child care policy issues. An important contribution of this paper is its thorough and detailed examination of current federal and state child care policy. Robins documents a pronounced shift in federal child care subsidies in recent years away from expenditure-based programs such as Title XX, that are targeted to low-income families, toward the Child Care Tax Credit, which benefits mainly middle- and upper-income families. He discusses the major recent legislative initiatives on child care, including the Family Support Act (FSA) and the recently passed package of new federal programs. Robins identifies the key policy issues concerning these recent child care initiatives as their costs, their labor supply effects, and their effects on the demand for child care. He then describes in detail how economists formulate models that can be used to analyze these issues, and reports the results of his own modeling efforts. His discussion is focused on the effects of making the Child Care Tax Credit refundable, which was an important element of the Act for Better Child Care Services (ABC) bill aimed at increasing the availability of the credit to low-income families. Robins concludes that the indirect costs of refundability may be quite large, because of increased use of the credit resulting from increased labor supply induced by refundability.

James Walker provides a different economic perspective on child care in "Public Policy and the Supply of Child Care Services." Using insights drawn from economic theory, together with detailed knowledge of the special characteristics of the child care market, Walker provides an analysis of the performance of the child care market in terms of economic efficiency. He describes popular perceptions of the child care market as a poorly functioning one characterized by chronic excess demand, low average quality of care, low wages, and high turnover. He notes that evaluation of these claims cannot be based on the simple descriptive statistics often used to support them, but rather requires an interpretive framework based on explicit models of consumer and provider behavior that incorporate specific features of the child care market. The specific features identified by Walker as important include the multidimensional nature of child care services, leading to product differentiation and the diversity of modes observed in the market; the often blurred distinction between consumers and producers, given that many child care providers are themselves mothers of young children; and the substantial differences between regulated and unregulated providers along dimensions such as education, experience, earnings, and firm size. Walker then provides an insightful analysis of possible sources of inefficiency in the child care market, discussing the consequences of imperfect information, incomplete markets, and externalities. Walker's paper is the first careful analysis of the child care market from a market organization perspective, and provides a wealth of useful insights on the issues involved in evaluating claims of market failure.

Rachel Connelly analyzes the demand side of the market for child care in her paper, "The Importance of Child Care Costs to Women's Decision Making." Connelly focuses on the influence of the cost of child care on labor supply behavior of mothers, a very important issue for public policy. If large new government subsidies to child care result in a lower net cost of care to families, more women are likely to enter the labor force, yielding a possibly large indirect cost to the government. Connelly uses the most recently available national data to provide a detailed analysis of who pays how much for child care. She makes the important point that a majority of families incur no direct cost for child care, and the determinants of whether a family makes any direct cash expenditures for child care may be different from the determinants of the level of expenditure among paying families. She also notes the importance of self-selection in data on child care expenditures: only families with employed mothers are included in the sample, but those mothers facing the highest cost for child care may have chosen not to work. After discussing these issues thoroughly, Connelly goes on to present a careful theoretical analysis of the impact of child care costs on fertility and employment decisions. She reviews the empirical literature on these subjects and concludes that there is a strong consensus among economists that child care costs exert a negative effect on labor force participation of mothers. There is not yet a consensus on the magnitude of the effect. Connelly identifies several important areas in which further research on this subject is needed.

The chapter written by Ellen Kisker and Rebecca Maynard, "Quality, Cost, and Parental Choice of Child Care," provides an analysis of the relationship between the quality and cost of child care, and how this influences parents' child care choices. The authors review evidence on the characteristics of child care that have been shown to be associated with good child development outcomes. They make the important point that parents may judge the quality of care by different criteria than those used by child development experts. It is argued that parents generally have very limited knowledge about the characteristics of their child care options that are important from a child development perspective. These points may help explain the fact that the price parents pay for child care tends to be unrelated to regulatable indicators of child care quality, despite the fact that the resource cost of child care is clearly related to these indicators. Kisker and Maynard identify several areas of public concern and describe the main policy options currently under consideration nationally. The likely effects of these options are reviewed, and the chapter concludes with a strong statement of support for policies to increase the availability and use of high quality care.

The last chapter in the volume, written by me, is "The Quality of Child Care: An Economic Perspective." This chapter has the goal of clarifying the difference between child development and economic views of child care quality. This may seem presumptuous on the part of an economist, given the expertise of members of the child development profession in measuring and analyzing factors that affect the well-being of children. However, child care choices are made by parents in the context of their preferences, budgets, and the regulatory environment, and these factors may have a decisive influence on the quality outcomes observed. In this paper I present simple characterizations of alternative models of child care quality and contrast their behavioral and policy implications. The "educator's" model focuses on the "technology" of producing child care quality and does not contain an active role for parents. The economic model contains the same "production process" as the educator's model, but embeds it in a model of family decision making. In this model, parents have preferences over child care quality as well as other attributes of child care arrangements such as convenience, reliability, and values shared with the provider. Empirical evidence concerning the implications of the economic model is reviewed, and some new evidence is presented on the determinants of the attributes of the inputs (child–staff ratio and provider training) in the child care arrangements chosen by families. The implications of the economic model for the current policy debate concerning federal regulations and tying increased subsidies to the use of regulated facilities are discussed.

The chapters in this volume (except my own) were originally papers presented at the Carolina Public Policy Conference on "The Economics of Child Care" held at the University of North Carolina at Chapel Hill on May 16, 1990. The conference was attended by about one hundred representatives of academic institutions, government agencies, think tanks, and citizen organizations. Each paper was discussed by an expert on child care from a field other than economics, including sociology, psychology, policy analysis, and advocacy. The comments of these experts contributed to a lively discussion at the conference and have been included here in written form when available.

2

Child Care Policy and Research: An Economist's Perspective

Philip K. Robins

Since the 1960s, the labor force participation rate of mothers of young children in the United States has been rising rapidly. As a consequence, policymakers have increasingly turned their attention to child care issues. In 1987, for example, more than seventy bills (representing close to fifty distinct pieces of legislation) were introduced into Congress with provisions for child care. In 1990, the first federal child care legislation since World War II was enacted. While a major step forward, many feel there is a further need for federal involvement. Although child care issues are complex and wide ranging, they appear to center around three notions: quality, availability, and affordability. In essence, the problem is one of ensuring access to decent and affordable child care for the more than 25 million children of working mothers. Because the child care needs of the population are so diverse, finding a long-lasting solution to this problem represents a significant national challenge.

Economists have recently discovered that they have much to contribute to the public debate on child care. Although child care research has a long history in sociology, psychology, and education, it is only recently that economists have begun seriously to address many of the central policy issues in this area. The purpose of this chapter is to describe the economic approach to child care and to show how economic research can be (and is being) used to shed light on several key child care policy issues.

FIGURE 1
LFP Rates for Married Women: 1970–1988

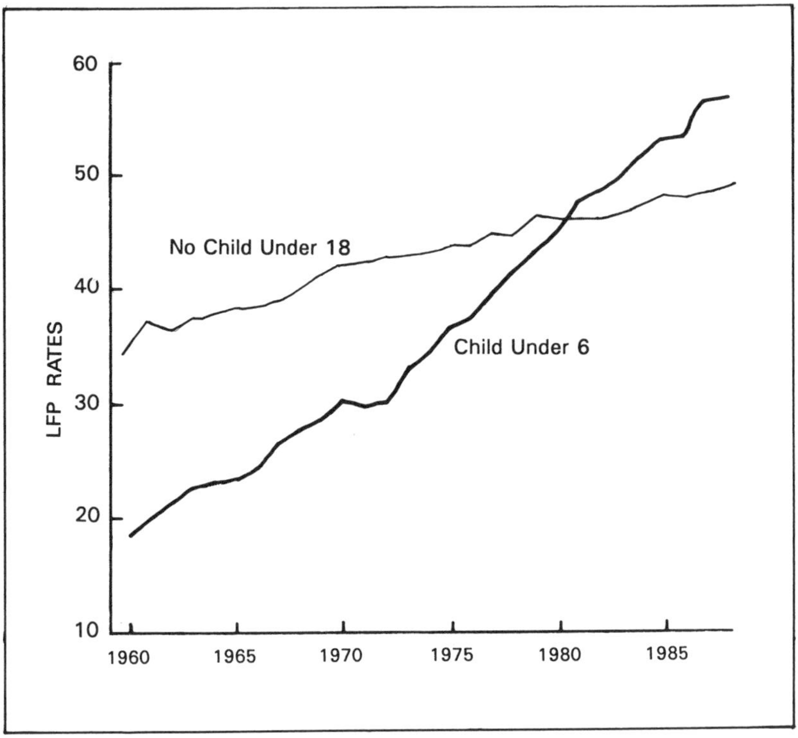

SOURCE: U.S. Department of Labor (1989).

FEMALE LABOR FORCE TRENDS

Ever since the turn of the century, labor force participation rates of women have been rising. However, as Figure 1 shows, since 1960 the rise has been most dramatic for married women with young children. In 1960, for example, the labor force participation rate of married women with children under age 6 was about one-half the rate for married women with no children under age 18 (18.6 percent versus 34.7 percent). By 1980, the rates were equal (46 percent), and by 1988 the rate for married women with young children exceeded the rate for married women without children by almost one-fifth (57.1 percent versus 48.9 percent). Between 1970 and 1988, the labor force participation rate of married women without children rose by 40.9 percent, while for married women with young children it rose by 135.5 percent.

Research has shown that a variety of factors is responsible for these trends. According to Bergmann (1986), the most important has been rising female wage rates. Other factors responsible for the trends include the introduction and widespread use of the contraceptive pill (O'Connell and Bloom 1987), the rising divorce rate (Johnson and Skinner 1986), the tremendous growth in the service sector of the economy relative to the goods sector, the reduction in stigma associated with leaving young children in the care of others, the desire to cushion economic shocks caused by an unexpected loss of a job, and government subsidization of child care costs.

While the labor force participation rate of women with young children has been rising in recent years, it is interesting to note that the percentage of all labor force participants with children has actually been declining. Tabulations from the Current Population Survey reported in Figure 2 indicate that parents repre-sented a *smaller* portion of the total labor force in 1985 than they did in 1968, despite significant increases in the labor force participation rate of women with children over this period. Such apparently contradicting trends are the result of a large influx of single persons into the labor force that has been swamping the increased labor force participation of mothers. Hence, although women have become a more dominant force in the labor market, parents have not. This may partially explain why the business sector has been slow in responding to the child care needs of working parents. For example, according to Hayghe (1988), only about 5 percent of the nation's 1.2 million nonagricultural estab-lishments with ten or more employees provided some form of direct child care assistance in 1987.[1] However, because of the aging of the population, the pool of prime-aged workers will be shrinking in the future and firms will likely be seeking ways (child care benefits being one of them) to induce greater numbers of young parents to join the labor force.

FEDERAL AND STATE POLICIES TOWARD CHILD CARE

The general indifference on the part of the business sector toward child care has intensified pressures on federal, state, and local governments to address the child care needs of working

---

[1] About 2 percent of these establishments sponsored day care centers and the other 3 percent provided financial assistance toward child care expenses. Indirect assistance was provided by another 11 percent of these establishments in the form of information and referral services, counseling services, and other services.

FIGURE 2
Composition of Labor Force: 1968–1985, by Presence of Children

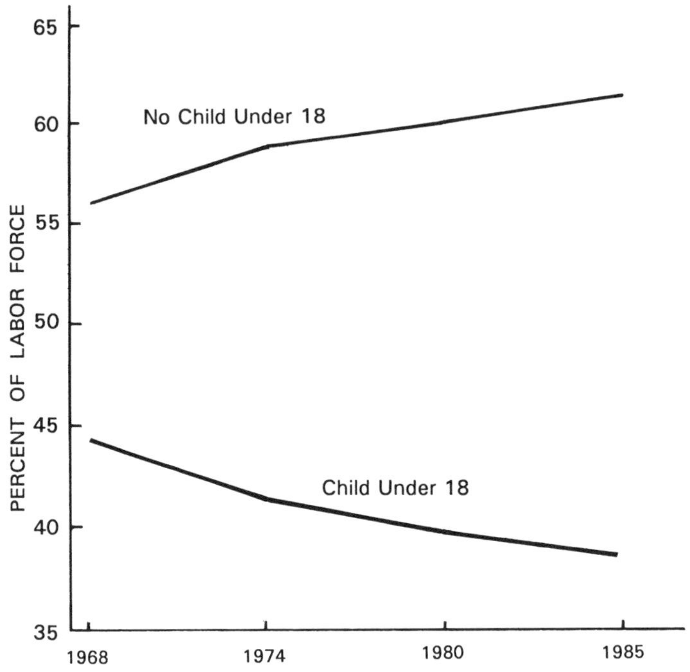

SOURCE: Tabulations from the 1968–1985 March Current Population Surveys, courtesy of William R. Prosser, U.S. Department of Health and Human Services.

parents. Currently, there are a wide variety of government programs that subsidize child care, but there is no coordinated policy at either the federal or state level. Furthermore, although government subsidies for child care have recently increased, most of the benefits have gone to middle- and upper-income families and the constant-dollar value of benefits for lower-income families has fallen.

Why Subsidize Child Care?

Before examining current federal and state policies with respect to child care, it is useful to ask the rather basic question,

"Why subsidize child care?" After all, it could be argued that child care is simply another commodity available for purchase by consumers and the decisions to have children, work, and purchase child care are all voluntary ones; therefore there is no economic justification for treating child care differently from other commodities.

This argument is deficient for two reasons. First, subsidization of child care may be cost-effective for the government. It can be argued that lack of adequate low-cost child care is a barrier to employment for many low-income persons receiving public assistance. By providing child care for low-income persons who are either working or in training, the dollar savings in future public assistance costs (due to increased earnings and eventual economic independence) may exceed the dollar costs of the child care being subsidized. Though no one has yet performed a formal study testing this conjecture, its validity is widely accepted among policymakers. In fact, it is a major reason the Family Support Act of 1988 contains a provision guaranteeing access to high quality child care for low-income families required to work or enroll in education or training programs.

But what about child care subsidies for families that are not receiving public assistance? One justification for these families is based on the argument that some working parents lack information about the quality of care their children are receiving and that this care may be of inadequate quality. Subsidization induces these parents to increase expenditures on child care and presumably increase the quality of care being purchased. Because quality child care has benefits that accrue to individuals beyond the family, government subsidization is warranted. Although the extent to which parents lack information about the quality of care their children are receiving is not known, nor is it known whether such care is actually of low quality relative to what is socially desirable, if society is risk averse, then subsidizing child care services purchased by families with working parents will make society better off. As will be argued below, one contribution economists can make to the child care debate concerning quality is to assess how government subsidization affects quality.

Federal Programs That Subsidize Child Care

The current system of federal support for child care is quite diverse and fragmented. The General Accounting Office (GAO) has identified forty-six separate federal programs that currently provide some form of child care-related assistance (U.S. GAO, 1989). The assistance is in the form of grants, services, scholarships, tax benefits, and agency-related child care activities.

One convenient way to classify child care programs is whether they are expenditure-based or tax-based. Expenditure-based programs are those encompassing direct spending on child care related activities. Tax-based programs are those in which the spending is in the form of reduced tax liabilities for consumers or businesses.

The expenditure- and tax-based programs identified by the GAO are listed in Table 1, along with the agency responsible for administering the program. As can be seen, the programs vary considerably in the type of assistance provided. It is worth noting that most of the programs provide very little assistance. According to the GAO, 89 percent of all federal spending on child care in 1988 was attributable to the four largest programs—the Child and Dependent Care Tax Credit, the Social Services Block Grant (Title XX), Head Start, and the Child Care Food Program—and more than half of all spending was attributable to the largest program, the Child and Dependent Care Tax Credit. About three-fifths of all federal spending is tax based, while the remainder is expenditure based.

Trends in Federal Spending

Figure 3 shows how federal spending (in constant 1988 dollars) changed under the thirteen largest programs from 1977 to 1988.[2] In 1977, about three-quarters of all federal spending was expenditure based. The largest source of federal funding for child care at that time was the Title XX program, which represented close to 40 percent of total spending. By 1988, however, Title XX represented only about 10 percent of total spending. There are two reasons for this dramatic change. First, the Omnibus Budget Reconciliation Act of 1981 (OBRA) amended Title XX to create the Social Service Block Grant, eliminating the separately funded

[2] The thirteen largest programs are the Social Services Block Grant Program (Title XX), Head Start, the Appalachian Child Development Program, the Child Care Food Program, the four Job Training Partnership Act Programs, the Aid to Families with Dependent Children Program (work expense disregard), the Work Incentive Program, the Food Stamp Program (dependent care deduction), the Dependent Care Assistance Program, and the Child and Dependent Care Tax Credit Program. These thirteen programs accounted for well over 90 percent of all federal spending on child care in 1988. The detailed figures underlying Figure 1 are presented in Robins (1990).

TABLE 1

Selected Federal Child Care Programs: 1988

Expenditure-based
1. Adult Education: Workplace Literacy Partnership (Education)
2. Aid to Families with Dependent Children (Health and Human Services)
3. Appalachian Child Development (Appalachian Regional Commission)
4. Business Development Assistance (Small Business Administration)
5. Census Bureau Surveys of Child Care Patterns (Commerce)
6. Child Care in Federal Buildings (General Services Administration)
7. Child Care Food Program (Agriculture)
8. Child Care in Military Institutions (Defense)
9. Child Development Associate Scholarships (Health and Human Services)
10. Child Welfare Research and Demonstration Projects (Health and Human Services)
11. Child Welfare Services State Grants (Health and Human Services)
12. Child Welfare Services Training Grants (Health and Human Services)
13. College Work-Study Program (Education)
14. Community Development Block Grants (Housing and Urban Development)
15. Community Services Block Grant (Health and Human Services)
16. Dependent Care Planning and Development (Health and Human Services)
17. Dislocated Workers Program (Labor)[a]
18. Economically Disadvantaged Individuals (Labor)[a]
19. Education of Handicapped Preschool Grant (Education)
20. Food Donation Program (Agriculture)
21. Food Stamps (Agriculture)
22. Guaranteed Student Loan Program (Education)
23. Head Start (Health and Human Services)
24. Indian Child Welfare Act
25. Job Corps (Labor)[a]
26. Migrant and Seasonal Farmworkers (Labor)[a]
27. Pell Grant Program (Education)
28. Perkins Loans (Education)
29. Public Housing (Housing and Urban Development)
30. Small Business Investment Companies (Small Business Administration)
31. Small Business Loans (Small Business Administration)
32. Social Services Block Grant, Title XX (Health and Human Services)
33. Special Milk Program for Children (Agriculture)
34. State Administrative Expenses for Child Nutrition (Agriculture)
35. State Student Incentive Grants (Education)
36. Summer Food Service Program for Children (Agriculture)
37. Supplemental Educational Opportunity Grants (Education)
38. Temporary Child Care for Handicapped Children (Health and Human Services)
39. Vocational Education (Education)
40. Women's Bureau (Labor)
41. Work Incentive Program (Labor, phased out in 1989)

TABLE 1 *(continued)*

Tax-based
1. Accelerated Cost Recovery System (Treasury)
2. Child and Dependent Care Tax Credit (Treasury)
3. Child Care as a Business Expense (Treasury)
4. Dependent Care Assistance Programs (Treasury)
5. Non-Profit Child Care Centers, Tax Exemption (Treasury)

SOURCE: U.S. General Accounting Office (1989).

*a*Funded under the Job Training Partnership Act.

Title XX social service program. Total Title XX funds were cut by about 20 percent, and states were given considerable flexibility in allocating program expenditures. As a consequence, federal Title XX spending for child care declined by almost 60 percent in constant dollars from 1977 to 1988. Second, over the same period, the Child Care Tax Credit expanded greatly, increasing by a factor of more than 7.5 from 1977 to 1988 (a factor of almost 4 in constant dollar terms). This expansion was the result of liberalized provisions and increased use by eligible families. By 1988, the Child Care Tax Credit had become the dominant form of government subsidization of child care, representing about 60 percent of all federal spending for child care, up from 25 percent in 1977. Because the tax credit is nonrefundable, meaning that it is limited to the amount of the individual's tax liability, the main beneficiaries have been middle- and upper-income families.

As Figure 3 indicates, federal spending for child care under expenditure-based programs declined by more than 13 percent in constant dollars from 1977 to 1988. Because most of the child care benefits accruing to low-income families are from expenditure-based programs, there has been a decided shift in the distribution of federal child care benefits.[3] Hence, although federal spending for child care has risen by almost 65 percent in constant dollar terms since 1977, virtually all the increased benefits have gone to middle- and upper-income families.

The increased spending for child care under the Child Care Tax Credit has been the result of more extensive use of the credit by the working population rather than greater subsidies per family. Table 2 shows how use of the credit has changed since its

[3]It has been estimated that 60 percent of all non-tax-related child care benefits accrue to low-income families (U.S. Congress 1978; Table 10). Because of nonrefundability, less than 1 percent of all tax-related child care benefits accrue to these families (U.S. Department of the Treasury 1985; Barnes 1988).

FIGURE 3
Federal Child Care Spending: 1977–1988, Constant 1988 Dollars

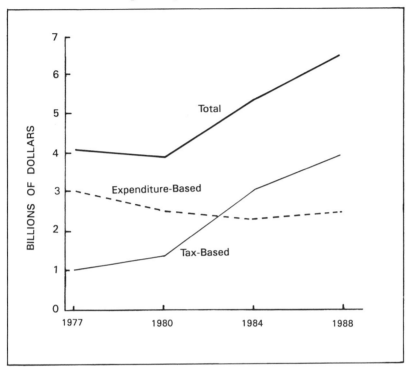

SOURCE: Robins (1990, Table 3).

inception in 1976.[4] First, in 1982, the tax credit was increased to 30 percent for low-income families and was reduced gradually on a sliding scale basis to 20 percent for families with incomes above $28,000. Before this the credit was a flat 20 percent for all families. Second, also in 1982, the maximum amount of child care expenses to which the credit could be applied was increased from $2,000 to $2,400 for one child and from $4,000 to $4,800 for two or more children. Third, and perhaps most importantly, in 1983 the credit was added to the short income tax form (1040A), which extended coverage to more low-income families.

As Table 2 indicates, the 1982 changes had only a minor effect on utilization of the credit, although they did significantly in-

---

[4] Prior to 1976, child care expenses were allowed as a deduction from income, but the subsidy was quite limited and available only to low-income families.

TABLE 2

Use of the Child Care Tax Credit: 1976–1988

Year	Number Claiming Credit (thousands)	Number Claiming Credit as a Percentage of Families with Working Mothers[a]	Total Amount of Credit ($ millions)[b]	Average Credit per Family[b]
1976	2,660	19.4%	$ 951	$358
1977	2,875	20.1	1,016	353
1978	3,431	22.7	1,185	346
1979	3,833	24.5	1,291	337
1980	4,231	25.6	1,371	324
1981	4,578	27.0	1,491	325
1982	5,004	30.0	1,838	367
1983	6,367	37.9	2,433	382
1984	7,546	42.4	3,016	400
1985	8,418	46.0	3,439	409
1986	8,950	47.3	3,668	410
1987	8,520	43.0	3,592	420
1988	8,992	44.7	3,803	423

SOURCES: U.S. Department of the Treasury (1976–1986, 1989); U.S. Department of Labor (1989).

[a] Working mothers with children under the age of 18.
[b] Expressed in 1988 dollars, using the Consumer Price Index.

crease the average credit per family (from $325 to $367 in 1988 dollars). The changes were not enough, however, to make up for the inflation that had occurred since the late 1970s. As Figure 4 indicates, though the credit was increased from 20 percent to 30 percent for low-income families, the maximum *constant dollar* benefit for this group was only 6 percent higher in 1982 than it was in 1976 ($1,763 in 1982 versus $1,660 in 1976). For middle- and upper-income families, the maximum constant dollar benefit fell by 29 percent (from $1,660 to $1,175), despite the increase in qualifying expenses. Hence, although the average credit per family in 1982 was 13 percent higher than in 1981, it was only 3 percent higher than in 1976. The addition of the short form in 1983 had a significant effect on the number of taxpayers using the credit, but had little effect on the size of the average credit.

Overall, then, from 1976 to 1988, child care subsidies through the Child Care Tax Credit increased by a factor of four in constant dollars. This increase came about primarily because of

FIGURE 4
*Maximum Child Care Tax Credit: 1976–1988,
Constant 1988 Dollars*

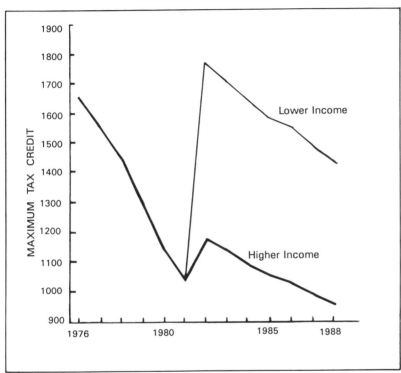

SOURCE: Robins (1990, Table 4).

more extensive use by eligible families. It is estimated that the percentage of families with working mothers using the credit increased from 19.4 percent in 1976 to 44.7 percent in 1987. In contrast, the average constant dollar credit per family increased by only about 18 percent from 1976 to 1988.

State Programs That Subsidize Child Care

The current system of state support for child care is also quite diverse and fragmented. As noted by the U.S. Department of Labor (1988), child care has had a long-established and well-developed system of support in some states, while in others it represents a new field of action. All states, however, currently provide some kind of child care assistance, either in the form of direct (expenditure based) or indirect (tax-based) spending, regulation of child care providers,[5] or support of resource and referral systems.

As shown in Table 3, twenty-eight states plus the District of Columbia currently subsidize child care through their tax codes. Of the remaining twenty-two states, eleven have an income tax but have chosen not to subsidize child care. The other eleven states do not have an income tax or have a very limited income tax that is applied to only certain types of unearned income. Figures are not currently available on the total value of these tax subsidies, but it probably falls in the range of 5 to 10 percent of the total federal subsidy.

Most of the state tax subsidies are tied to the federal Child Care Tax Credit. In some states (California), the credit is as low as 5 percent of the federal credit, whereas in others (Kansas, Minnesota) it is as high as 100 percent of the federal tax credit. Seven states treat child care expenses as a deduction from income, which as indicated above is similar to how the federal subsidy operated before 1976. In these seven states, taxpayers are subsidized at a rate equal to the tax bracket into which they fall. Three states (Alaska, New Mexico, and Minnesota) have a refundable tax credit, which facilitates access to the credit for low-income families. As will be seen below, a refundable tax credit is currently being proposed at the federal level.

Besides the three states with a refundable tax credit, low-income families are subsidized mainly through the Social Services Block Grant Program (Title XX). However, four states (Alaska, California, Montana, and Oregon) use only state funds to subsidize child care for low-income families. Fifteen states provide funds to support resource and referral programs and nineteen states provide funds for day care centers used by state employees. Other state support includes funds for training child care workers. One state (California) jointly channels funds with the private sector to recruit, train, and provide technical assistance to child care providers (the California Child Care Initiative).

Separate state figures are not available for spending on child care services under the Social Services Block Grant program and

---

[5]There are currently no federal regulations for child care providers. The Federal Interagency Day Care Regulations, originally formulated in 1968, were eliminated with the passage of the Omnibus Budget Reconciliation Act of 1981.

TABLE 3

State Child Care Tax Subsidy Programs: 1988[a]

State	Description of Program	Phase Out with Income	Maximum Subsidy
Alabama	None	—	—
Alaska	.16 of Federal Credit[a,b]	No	$ 230
Arizona	Tax ded. for child care exp.	Yes	$ 39
Arkansas	.10 of Federal Credit	No	$ 144
California	.05 to .10 of Federal Credit	No	$ 144
Colorado	Tax ded. for child care exp.	No	$ 384
Connecticut	None[c]	—	—
Delaware	.25 of Federal Credit	No	$ 360
District of Columbia	.30 of Federal Credit	No	$ 432
Florida	None[d]	—	—
Georgia	Tax credit for child care exp.	No	$ 80
Hawaii	.10 of child care expenses	No	$ 200
Idaho	Tax ded. for child care exp.	No	$ 360
Illinois	None	—	—
Indiana	None[e]	—	—
Iowa	.45 of Federal Credit	No	$ 648
Kansas	.1 to 1.0 of Federal Credit	No	$ 162
Kentucky	Credit based on no. of child.	No	$ 400
Louisiana	.10 of Federal Credit	No	$ 144
Maine	.25 of Federal Credit	No	$ 360
Maryland	Tax deduction for child care	Yes	$ 240
Massachusetts	Tax deduction for child care	No	$ 240
Michigan	None	—	—
Minnesota	Tax credit for child care exp.[b]	Yes	$1,440
Mississippi	None	—	—
Missouri	None	—	—
Montana	Tax ded. for child care exp.	Yes	$ 528
Nebraska	None	—	—
Nevada	None[d]	—	—
New Hampshire	None[c]	—	—
New Jersey	None	—	—
New Mexico	Tax credit for child care exp.[b]	No	$1,200
New York	.20 of Federal Credit	Yes	$ 288
North Carolina	Credit for child care expenses	Yes	$ 336
North Dakota	None	—	—
Ohio	.25 of Federal Credit	No	$ 360
Oklahoma	.20 of Federal Credit	No	$ 288
Oregon	.40 of Federal Credit	No	$ 576
Pennsylvania	None	—	—
Rhode Island	.22 of Federal Credit	No	$ 320
South Carolina	.07 of Federal Credit	No	$ 101
South Dakota	None[d]	—	—
Tennessee	None[c]	—	—
Texas	None[d]	—	—

TABLE 3   *(continued)*

State	Description of Program	Phase Out with Income	Maximum Subsidy
Utah	None	—	—
Vermont	.265 of Federal Credit	No	$ 382
Virginia	Tax deduction for child care	Yes	$ 276
Washington	None[d]	—	—
West Virginia	None	—	—
Wisconsin	None[f]	—	—
Wyoming	None[d]	—	—

SOURCES: U.S. Department of Labor (1988); unpublished data provided by David Blau, University of North Carolina.

[a] Suspended until January 1993.
[b] Tax credit is refundable.
[c] State has a very limited income tax that is applied only to unearned income.
[d] State does not have an income tax.
[e] Five-cent cigarette tax used to fund child care programs.
[f] A tax credit equal to .3 of federal credit was repealed in 1985.

other state and local programs. However, the American Public Welfare Association conducted a survey of the states and obtained estimates of combined federal, state, and local spending for child care services in each state for 1985 (American Public Welfare Association, 1988). These estimates are presented in Table 4. To give a better perspective for comparable spending across states, spending per child under age 18 is also presented in Table 4. States are ranked by both aggregate and per child spending.

As Table 4 indicates, total federal, state, and local spending for child care services in 1985 was approximately $1.1 billion. The five states spending the most were California, New York, Pennsylvania, Massachusetts, and Illinois. Together, these states accounted for close to three-fifths of all federal, state, and local spending. The five states spending the least were Idaho, Nevada, South Dakota, Wyoming, and Montana. On a per capita basis, the rankings were generally similar to the aggregate rankings, although the District of Columbia, which ranked seventeenth in total spending, ranked first in per capita spending, and Illinois, which ranked fifth in total spending, ranked twentieth in per capita spending.

As indicated above, federal spending on Title XX in recent years has been about 10 percent of total federal spending on child care. In 1985, federal Title XX spending was about $550 million. Thus, it appears that the states contributed about $550 million

TABLE 4

State Spending on Child Care Services: 1985[a]

State	Expenditures (millions)	Expenditures per Child Under 18	Rank (expenditures)	Rank (expenditures per child)
Alabama	$ 10.5	$ 9.36	23	30
Alaska	$ 1.0	$ 5.88	45	37
Arizona	$ 15.6	$ 17.81	16	8
Arkansas	$ 3.1	$ 4.73	38	41
California	$325.8	$ 47.71	1	2
Colorado	$ 10.3	$ 11.95	24	22
Connecticut	$ 12.7	$ 16.79	20	10
Delaware	$ 2.5	$ 15.95	40	12
Dist. of Columbia	$ 14.2	$108.38	17	1
Florida	$ 36.3	$ 14.32	8	13
Georgia	$ 23.4	$ 14.15	11	15
Hawaii	$ 2.5	$ 8.63	39	31
Idaho	$ 0.2	$ 0.55	51	51
Illinois	$ 39.0	$ 12.58	5	20
Indiana	$ 8.6	$ 5.71	25	38
Iowa	$ 1.8	$ 2.27	43	47
Kansas	$ 3.1	$ 4.69	36	42
Kentucky	$ 6.9	$ 6.70	30	36
Louisiana	$ 13.0	$ 9.58	18	26
Maine	$ 4.0	$ 13.17	34	19
Maryland	$ 18.1	$ 16.51	13	11
Massachusetts	$ 53.0	$ 38.91	4	3
Michigan	$ 23.8	$ 9.58	10	27
Minnesota	$ 16.2	$ 14.19	15	14
Mississippi	$ 6.2	$ 7.81	31	33
Missouri	$ 7.5	$ 5.65	28	39
Montana	$ 0.5	$ 2.13	47	49
Nebraska	$ 3.3	$ 7.39	35	34
Nevada	$ 0.2	$ 1.06	50	50
New Hampshire	$ 3.1	$ 12.31	37	21
New Jersey	$ 37.1	$ 19.94	7	6
New Mexico	$ 4.2	$ 9.37	33	29
New York	$141.3	$ 32.31	2	4
N. Carolina	$ 17.0	$ 10.70	14	23
N. Dakota	$ 0.7	$ 3.43	46	44
Ohio	$ 30.3	$ 10.57	9	24
Oklahoma	$ 18.2	$ 19.72	12	7
Oregon	$ 1.9	$ 2.66	42	46
Pennsylvania	$ 70.4	$ 24.42	3	5
Rhode Island	$ 1.2	$ 5.28	44	40
S. Carolina	$ 12.8	$ 13.89	19	17
S. Dakota	$ 0.4	$ 2.18	49	48
Tennessee	$ 8.5	$ 6.93	26	35
Texas	$ 37.7	$ 7.86	6	32

TABLE 4 *(continued)*

State	Expenditures (millions)	Expenditures per Child Under 18	Rank (expenditures)	Rank (expenditures per child)
Utah	$ 8.5	$ 13.90	27	16
Vermont	$ 2.4	$ 17.40	41	9
Virginia	$ 5.3	$ 3.66	32	43
Washington	$ 11.3	$ 9.57	22	28
West Virginia	$ 7.0	$ 13.53	29	18
Wisconsin	$ 12.4	$ 9.64	21	25
Wyoming	$ 0.5	$ 3.12	48	45
Total	$1,095	$ 17.39		

SOURCE: Adapted from American Public Welfare Association (1988).

NOTE: The population figures used to derive expenditures per child were taken from the Statistical Abstract of the United States.

[a]Includes federal, state, and local spending for the fiscal year.

of their own funds for child care in 1985. If state tax subsidies for child care were 10 percent of the federal subsidy at that time (which is probably an upper bound), then another $350 million of state funds were spent on child care subsidies. Thus, in 1985, it appears the states were spending about, at most, $900 million on child care, or approximately 20 percent of the federal total.

Regulation of Child Care Facilities

Although there are currently no federal regulations governing child care facilities, each state has developed a varying set of standards. As indicated by the U.S. General Accounting Office (1989), all states regulate child care centers through licensing provisions,[6] and forty-eight states regulate family care arrangements through licensing or registration. About half the states with regulations for family care arrangements have traditional licensing, a third have mandatory registration, a few have either registration or licensing only of subsidized facilities, and the rest have voluntary registration.

The standards for regulation vary widely. Some states require child–staff ratios as low as 3 to 1, whereas others allow a ratio of 20 to 1. Maximum group sizes range from 4 to 20 or more.

[6]Many states exempt from licensing requirements centers run by religious institutions.

These maximum child–staff ratios and group sizes generally vary with the age of the child.

RECENT LEGISLATIVE PROPOSALS

Since 1987, child care legislation has been introduced at a frenetic pace at both the federal and state levels. In 1987 alone, more than seventy bills (representing close to fifty distinct pieces of legislation) were introduced into Congress.[7] Many of these bills called for increased spending under existing programs; others created new programs.

The most comprehensive bill introduced in 1987 was the Act for Better Child Care Services (ABC). It called for $2.5 billion per year to fund a broad range of child care services. This bill was supported by more than one hundred national activist groups (members of a coalition known as the Alliance for Better Child Care) and had more than two hundred cosponsors in both houses of Congress. Although the original ABC bill did not become law, it became the basis for legislation included as part of the Omnibus Budget Reconciliation Act of 1990.

The 1990 legislation is particularly noteworthy in that it authorizes additional spending of $22 billion during a five-year period in which the overall federal budget is to be trimmed by $492 billion. As Table 5 indicates, the child care funds are to be distributed through a child care block grant ($2.5 billion), an expansion of the Earned Income Tax Credit ($12.4 billion), a refundable tax credit for families with children under the age of one ($.7 billion),[8] a child health tax credit ($5.2 billion), and child care assistance to mothers on welfare ($1.5 billion).

One other major piece of legislation has been enacted into law recently that provides significant federal child care aid. This is the Family Support Act of 1988 (FSA). One provision of the FSA establishes the JOBS program, which requires welfare recipients to enroll in work or training programs as a condition of receiving benefits. The act specifically stipulates that child care services must be provided to recipients participating in the JOBS program. The legislation also provides up to twelve months of transitional

---

[7] A listing and description of these bills are given in an unpublished appendix to Robins (1990).

[8] This new refundable tax credit for families with children under the age of one will not be available to families choosing to utilize the existing nonrefundable dependent-care tax credit.

TABLE 5

Child Care Legislation Enacted in 1990

I. Child Care and Development Block Grant
$750 million FY 1991
$825 million FY 1992
$925 million FY 1993
As necessary FY 1994, 1995
  A. State allocation formula
    Number of children under 5
    Number of children participating in school lunch program
    Per capita income
  B. State match
    None
  C. Allocation of funds
    75% direct payments to parents for child care
    25% improving existing programs
  D. Standards
    Must establish health and safety requirements
    Requirements may be more stringent for participating providers
    One-time review of licensing policies and regulations
  E. Eligibility
    Child must be under 13
    Family can earn at most 75% of state median income
II. Social Security Block Grant
  $1.5 billion to aid parents on AFDC
III. Tax Credits
  A. Earned Income Tax Credit
    Increased by $12.4 billion over 5 years
  B. Refundable Child Tax Credit
    $.7 billion for low-income families with children under the
    age of 1
  C. Child Health Tax Credit
    $5.2 billion for low-income families paying health insurance
    premiums

SOURCE: Child Care Action Campaign (1990).

child care aid to welfare recipients who leave the rolls as a result of becoming gainfully employed.

KEY POLICY ISSUES IN CHILD CARE

Virtually all the recent child care initiatives attempt to address the problems of affordability, availability, and quality of child care. As indicated earlier, one economic justification for a greater federal role in child care is based on the assumption that, under the existing system, an inadequate amount of high quality child care is being purchased by families with working parents. Another justification is that child care subsidies can reduce welfare costs by facilitating employment among welfare recipients.

Thus, child care subsidies are expected to increase employment of welfare recipients and increase the quality of child care being purchased by families with working parents by making higher quality care more affordable. Although these effects appear reasonable, very little empirical evidence exists confirming their validity. It is therefore of great interest to provide credible estimates of whether such effects are likely to occur.

One additional policy consideration currently creating controversy among policymakers concerns the costs of child care legislation. As indicated earlier, the recently enacted child care bill is estimated to cost $22 billion over the next five years. Estimating the costs of child care programs can be very difficult because of the economic effects they are likely to generate. For example, many child care analysts support a refundable child care tax credit to increase equity in the distribution of federal child care benefits (see, for example, Robins 1988). Although not included in the final version of the recently enacted federal child care legislation, a refundable child care tax credit had been part of the original bill.[9] The costs of converting to a refundable tax credit are both direct and indirect. The direct costs include the reduced taxes for persons currently ineligible for the credit, because it is nonrefundable. The indirect costs include the additional credits arising from families spending more on child care because of the availability of the increased subsidy. However, to the extent that the subsidy induces more work effort, tax revenues may also increase (because of the increased earnings). Thus, the net indirect costs may be positive or negative.[10]

The key policy issues surrounding recent child care initiatives concern their cost, their effects on the work behavior of family members, and their effects on the quality and amount of child care purchased in the market. As is argued below, economists can contribute a great deal toward resolving these issues.

[9] Recall that the 1990 legislation does include a refundable child tax credit. However, the credit is not tied to expenditures on child care and is restricted to families with children under the age of one.

[10] Current government estimates of the costs of the various child care bills do not include the indirect costs. The indirect costs are very difficult to calculate because they require knowledge of the size of the economic effects generated by the legislation *before it is actually implemented.*

THE ROLE OF ECONOMIC RESEARCH
IN ANALYZING KEY CHILD CARE POLICY ISSUES

As the public debate on child care takes center stage, numerous economists are turning their attention to developing ways of helping policymakers address the key policy issues. The economic approach to analyzing child care issues consists of three steps: (1) developing an economic model, (2) empirically estimating the economic model, and (3) using the results to analyze policy issues.

Developing an Economic Model

For economic analysis to be a useful tool for analyzing child care policy issues, an economic model must be specified. The model must be relevant, that is, it must directly incorporate factors associated with the policy issues. For purposes of the discussion here, suppose the government is interested in determining whether a refundable child care tax credit will facilitate labor force participation of mothers and increase the quality of child care purchased in the market. Also, suppose there is interest in whether a refundable credit would be more equitable than the existing credit and whether tax revenues would go up or down as a result of a refundable credit.

These issues can be analyzed using a simple economic model of family behavior.[11] The model is based on the assumption that family members make choices regarding consumption of child care quality, consumption of market goods other than child care, and consumption of leisure (time spent not working). The choices are made to maximize family well-being. More specifically, it is assumed that parents derive utility (or satisfaction) from consumer goods, child care quality, and leisure time. The quality of child care is a combination of the quality of care provided by the parents and the quality of care provided by others while the parents work. Care provided by others can be "free" care, provided by relatives and friends, or care purchased in the market (day care center, hired sitter, family day care home, or the like).

---

[11] The discussion that follows is based on the models developed in Blau and Robins (1988) and Michalopoulos, Robins, and Garfinkel (1990).

The economic model of family behavior makes no presumption about whether the quality of child care purchased in the market or provided by others is less than, equal to, or greater than the quality of child care provided by the parents. Families that strongly desire consumer goods may be willing to sacrifice child care quality to satisfy their consumption desires. On the other hand, each family sets a "minimum" acceptable quality of child care. This "minimum" quality of child care varies across families and may be less than or equal to the quality of care provided by the parents. It may also be less than, equal to, or greater than the quality of care recommended by child development experts. If the "minimum" quality of care equals the quality of care provided by the parents or the quality of care recommended by experts, then the parents would never purchase care in the market that is of lower quality than these amounts. On the other hand, if the "minimum" quality of care is less than the quality of parental care or the quality of care recommended by experts, then the family may indeed purchase care in the market that is of lower quality than these amounts.[12]

In the economic model, each family chooses overall child care quality, the amount of time to work, and the amount of consumer goods to purchase to achieve the highest level of family well-being. The model is solved mathematically for the optimum amounts of these variables as functions of their "exogenous" determinants, which include the price of child care, the wage rates of the parents, family nonwage income, and demographic characteristics of the families that may be related to their tastes.

Two important conditions that must be satisfied in the economic model of family behavior are (1) that a family spend money on consumer goods and child care to equalize its subjective evaluation of the "marginal" utility of the last dollar spent on these goods, and (2) that the loss in utility from an additional hour of work is exactly offset by the gain in utility from the additional consumption of market goods made possible by the additional earnings plus the loss (or gain) in utility from substituting nonparental child care for parental child care.

---

[12] The important point to emphasize here is that the economic model is designed to explain actual preferences and choices regarding child care quality, not the preferences or choices deemed appropriate by child development experts or other individuals concerned with the well-being of children.

Estimating the Economic Model

The optimal conditions above translate into a set of mathematical equations that describe family behavior. These "structural" equations will contain unknown "parameters" that describe the intensity of the relationship between the "exogenous" variables (price of child care, wage rates, income, demographic characteristics) and the "endogenous" choice variables (child care quality, purchases of consumer goods, and the amount of time that the parents spend working). If the assumptions of the model are valid, then the parameters can be estimated by applying statistical techniques such as regression analysis to real world microlevel data on the exogenous and endogenous variables.

The parameters of this type of structural model have been estimated by Michalopoulos, Robins, and Garfinkel (1990), using data from the Survey of Income and Program Participation (SIPP) for the winter of 1984–1985.[13] The SIPP is a national survey in which parents are asked about their child care expenditures, work behavior, and other socioeconomic information. Their analysis sample consisted of about 4,700 two-parent families and 1,600 single-parent families.

Because child care quality was not observed in the data, it was necessary to make a further assumption to identify the various qualities of child care defined by the model. The assumption made was that the quality of child care purchased in the market can be approximated by the reported level of child care expenditures.[14] By making this assumption, it was possible to identify the quality of parental care and the minimum acceptable quality of care.

Some of the main findings of this study are given in Table 6. It should be noted that these findings apply to families in which

---

[13] "Structural" estimates of an economic model are much more closely tied to an underlying theoretical framework than are "reduced form" estimates. Structural estimates are also better suited for generalization, but they are more sensitive to specification errors than are reduced form estimates. For reduced form estimates of an economic model of child care, see Blau and Robins (1988).

[14] In the economic model, child care quality may embrace characteristics that differ from those recommended by child development experts. For example, some parents may be more willing to pay for child care that is "convenient" as opposed to that having a low "child–staff ratio." Thus, even if parents spend as much on child care as is recommended by child development experts, the care may not have the same characteristics, and in fact may not even meet the standards set by the experts. For an excellent discussion of how the "economic" and "educator" views toward child care quality differ, see Blau (this volume).

TABLE 6

*Estimated Quality of Child Care
and Its Responsiveness to Changes in Family Income* ·

	Married Mothers	Single Mothers
Quality of Mother's Care[a]	1.89	1.98
Minimum Acceptable Quality[a]	1.55	1.56
Quality of Purchased Care[a]	1.52	1.05
Responsiveness to an Increase		
(1) In the Mother's Wage[b]		
Hours of work	.002	.032
Quality of purchased care	.138	.488
Total child care expenditures	.145	.562
(2) In Other Family Income[c]		
Hours of work	−.001	−.019
Quality of purchased care	.278	.072
Total child care expenditures	.278	.046
(3) In Child Care Subsidies[d]		
Hours of work	.0001	.002
Quality of purchased care	.247	.129
Total child care expenditures	.247	.141

SOURCE: Michalopolous, Robins, and Garfinkel (1990).

[a] Measured in dollars per hour (April 1990 dollars).
[b] Measured as an elasticity, which is the percent change resulting from a 1 percent change in the wage.
[c] Measured as an elasticity, which is the percent change resulting from a 1 percent change in other family income.
[d] Measured as an elasticity, which is the percent change resulting from a 1 percent change in the combined federal and state child care subsidy rates.

the mother works and child care is purchased in the market. The findings indicate that the estimated average quality of parental care for these families is between 22 and 27 percent higher than the minimum acceptable quality of care to the family. The average quality of care purchased in the market is between 20 and 53 percent lower than the quality of parental care and between 2 and 33 percent lower than the minimum acceptable care.[15] Expenditures on child care increase with the wage rate of the mother, other family income, and child care subsidies.[16] Virtu-

[15] Even though the quality of purchased care is less than the minimum acceptable quality of care, the *average* quality of care provided for the child (which is a weighted average of parental care plus purchased care) exceeds the minimum quality care for virtually all the families.

[16] The child care subsidies considered in the study are those associated with the federal and state child care tax credit programs. An increase in subsidies is equivalent to a reduction in the price of child care.

ally all the increase is the result of higher quality child care being purchased (more expenditures per hour) rather than more hours of child care being used (due to longer hours of work).[17]

The finding that families generally purchase low quality child care confirms the suspicions of many policymakers. Furthermore, the finding that child care quality and expenditures increased in response to child care subsidies suggests that recent legislative proposals to increase child care subsidies should lead to an increase in child care quality. The results of this study can be used to predict how much quality would increase if the new legislation was enacted.

How the Results Can Be Used to Analyze Key Policy Issues

Once estimates of the economic model have been obtained, the results can be used to analyze key policy issues. One approach to analyzing these issues that has proven useful in similar contexts is microsimulation analysis. Microsimulation analysis utilizes the economic behavioral relationships together with program rules to predict the effects of a given child care policy. The predictions are made by "simulating" the policy for a sample of families. For example, suppose we are interested in both the direct and indirect effects of making the child care tax credit refundable. The direct effects are obtained by applying the program rules to a sample of families, but keeping family behavior at the preprogram levels. Thus, the direct effects of making the tax credit refundable would be determined by estimating how much additional credit would be taken if the tax credit were refundable, without allowing work effort, child care expenditures, and other consumption expenditures to change in response to the program. The indirect effects would be obtained by predicting how work effort, child care expenditures, and other consumption expenditures would change in response to the program, and then calculating the additional credit at the new levels of these outcome variables.[18]

---

[17] Because the responses in Table 6 are conditional on working and purchasing child care in the market, they do not capture effects on the decision to work or purchase child care.

[18] It should be noted that, in principle, other aspects of family behavior may change in response to the child care policy. For example, making the child care tax credit refundable may induce additional births. To simulate these types of changes would require a more comprehensive economic model that treats family structure as "endogenous." For a discussion of the effects of child care policy on family structure, see Blau and Robins (1989).

To date, only one study has simulated both the direct and indirect effects of child care policies using a structural model (Michalopoulos et al. 1990).[19] Figure 5 presents their estimates for two versions of a refundable tax credit. The first version simply makes the existing tax credit refundable. The second version is a proposal I made (see Robins 1988; 1990) which, in addition to making the credit refundable, makes it more progressive by increasing the credit percentage for low-income families from 30 percent to 80 percent, and gradually phasing out the credit to zero at incomes above $60,000, compared to the current credit, which phases down to 20 percent at incomes above $28,000. I believe this version of a refundable credit would go much farther than simple refundability because it would better satisfy what I consider to be the most important objectives of a national child care policy, namely *flexibility* (not tying benefits to any one particular child care arrangement), *equity* (giving poorer families a proportionately greater share of the benefits), *simplicity* (eliminating the complex overlapping of many programs), and *target efficiency* (maximizing the percentage of program funds going directly to families).

As Figure 5 indicates, only about one-quarter of the benefits under the existing credit go to the bottom half of the income distribution. Making the credit refundable would make it far more equitable (about 43 percent of the benefits would go to the bottom half of the income distribution). Making the credit more progressive as well as refundable would tilt benefits even farther to lower-income families (about half of the benefits would go to the bottom half of the income distribution). Michalopoulos et al. find that a large portion of the increased subsidies given to families are the result of indirect (behavioral) effects.

In addition to the distributional effects, Michalopoulos et al. also estimated the direct and indirect costs of these proposed changes in the child care tax credit. They find that about two-thirds of the additional costs of a refundable credit are the result of behavioral responses, and about four-fifths of the additional costs of a more progressive credit are the result of behavioral responses. A refundable credit is estimated to increase total costs by about one-third, and a more progressive credit is estimated to increase total costs by about a factor of eight. The large behav-

---

[19] Henderson (1989) considers the indirect costs using a reduced form model applied to aggregate data. He finds that more than half of each additional dollar of tax credit is offset by increased tax revenues due to additional earnings.

FIGURE 5
Altering the Child Care Tax Credit,
Direct and Indirect Distributional Effects

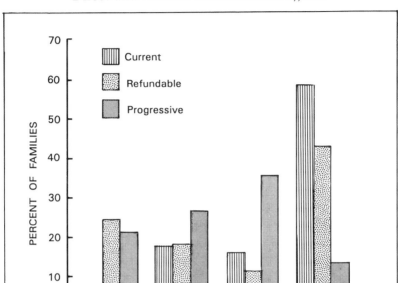

SOURCE: Michalopoulos, Robins, and Garfinkel (1990).

ioral effects of the more progressive credit are due to both the significant estimated sensitivity on the part of families to price reductions and the large price reduction implied by more progressive credit.[20]

Additional Considerations

There are at least two additional considerations that must be taken into account in evaluating the economic effects of changes in child care policy. One has to do with whether or not the supply of child care services can expand in response to the

[20] The analysis by Blau and Robins (1989) suggests that the proposed changes in the child care tax credit would also increase the number of children born, which would further increase costs and distributional effects.

changes in family behavior predicted by the economic model; the other has to do with institutional constraints that may prevent families from behaving in the manner predicted by the economic model.

The economic model discussed above assumes that the supply of child care services can expand in response to increases in the demand for child care services without an increase in the average cost of child care. If supply cannot expand in this manner, then the cost of providing child care services would rise and the amount of services produced would not increase enough to provide child care to all the families who would like it at the original average cost. In economic terms, this effect will depend on the "price elasticity" of the supply of child care services. If the price elasticity is very large, then supply can increase with no corresponding increase in the cost of child care services. If the price elasticity is very small, then supply cannot increase by very much and the cost of child care services would correspondingly rise.

There is some evidence that the supply of child care services can increase by the amount of the increased demand, without a corresponding increase in the cost of care. For example, a recent study by Blau (1989) finds that the supply of child care services is highly price-elastic. A study by Prosser (1986) finds that, from 1976 to 1984, the supply of day care centers increased more than the number of young children who have mothers in the labor force. During the same period, Hofferth (1987) reports that the cost of day care center care remained roughly constant, suggesting a very high price elasticity of supply.

The other consideration has to do with whether or not institutional constraints would prevent families from actually behaving in the manner predicted by the economic model. Consider the case of a refundable tax credit. Because the current credit is not refundable, it is not really known whether low-income families would actually use the credit if it were available to them. For example, it has been argued that because of the way the tax system is structured, families would not benefit from the credit until they filed their tax returns, and thus they might be unable to meet monthly (or even weekly) child care expenses (U.S. Congress 1985). However, this problem could possibly be avoided by using the existing withholding system to meet monthly child care needs.[21]

---

[21] See Robins (1990) for a detailed discussion of how the withholding system can be used to help low-income families meet child care expenses on a timely basis.

It has also been argued that most low-income families cannot afford to purchase child care in the open market (that is, from child care centers or licensed family day care homes). Instead, they tend to rely upon in-home babysitters or out-of-home arrangements that are usually unlicensed (and, hence, illegal), and pay less than minimum wages to caretakers who do not declare their income for social security purposes (U.S. Commission on Civil Rights 1981). However, a very generous refundable credit, perhaps at 80 percent for very low-income families, is likely to induce many of these families to seek higher quality (licensed) arrangements, and many caretakers might also then seek licenses and declare their income for tax purposes.

Finally, it has been argued that the tax credit encourages widespread cheating because it is difficult to verify claimed expenses (Besharov 1988). Although this argument has some merit, cheating can be effectively controlled by requiring certification of providers and limiting the credit to families that utilize certified providers. It may be noted that the recently enacted Family Support Act has instituted just such a provision in the current tax credit law.

CONCLUDING COMMENTS

Current public policy toward child care is undergoing rapid change. No longer at issue is the question of whether a significant amount of government assistance is necessary to help ensure access to affordable, adequate child care for the millions of children of working parents. This is evidenced by recent legislation enacted in the face of intense efforts to trim the federal budget deficit. The only remaining issues of concern and debate have to do with the form and the amount of the assistance.

Economists have a great deal to contribute to the current child care debate. Economic analysis can identify where the current child care system is lacking and can provide scientifically based estimates of how proposed child care reforms can alleviate the problems facing the current system. The power of economic analysis is that it can evaluate alternative policies before they are actually implemented and hence can contribute to the efficient allocation of public resources.

At this time, economic analysis of child care issues is in its infancy. There is considerable need for further development of economic models of family behavior that can deal effectively with the wide range of behavioral phenomena affected by child care policy. In addition, there is also a great need for building realistic simulation models capable of predicting the behavioral effects of both expenditure-based and tax-based child care programs.

Although economic analysis is a powerful tool for analyzing the effects of child care policies, it is not without its limitations. There are many factors that cannot be considered by an economic model and which are critical for understanding the implications of a particular child care policy. To be most effective, economic analysis must be used in conjunction with the analyses of sociologists, psychologists, demographers, educators, and other child care researchers. The combined insights of all these disciplines are needed to advance the development of policies that will ultimately better serve our nation's children.

This is a revised version of a paper presented at the Carolina Public Policy Conference, May 16, 1990. The author would like to thank David Blau and William Prosser for helpful comments.

REFERENCES

American Public Welfare Association. 1988. "Analysis of Child Welfare Services Expenditure Data and Child Day Care Expenditure Data." Report submitted to the Assistant Secretary for Planning and Evaluation, Department of Health and Human Services, September.

Barnes, Roberta Ott. 1988. "The Distributional Effects of Alternative Child Care Proposals." Paper presented at the tenth annual meeting of the Association for Public Policy and Management, October.

Bergmann, Barbara R. 1986. *The Economic Emergence of Women.* New York: Basic Books.

Besharov, Douglas J. 1988. Testimony before the Senate Finance Committee, September 22.

Blau, David M. 1989. "The Labor Market Effects of Child Care Subsidies." Unpublished manuscript. University of North Carolina at Chapel Hill, April.

Blau, David M., and Philip K. Robins. 1989. "Fertility, Employment, and Child Care Costs." *Demography* 26, 2(May):287–299.

————. 1988. "Child Care Costs and Family Labor Supply." *Review of Economics and Statistics* 70, 3(August):374–381.

Child Care Action Campaign. 1990. Child Care Action News, Vol. 7, No. 6, p. 3, New York.

Hayghe, Howard. 1988. "Employers and Child Care: What Roles Do They Play." *Monthly Labor Review* (September):38–44.

Henderson, David R. 1989. "The Supply-Side Tax Revenue Effects of the Child Care Tax Credit." *Journal of Policy Analysis and Management* 8, 4(Fall):673–675.

Hofferth, Sandra L. 1987. "Child Care in the United States." Statement before the House Select Committee on Children, Youth, and Families, July 1.

Johnson, William R., and Jonathan Skinner. 1986. "Labor Supply and Marital Separation." *American Economic Review* 76, 3(June):455–469.

Michalopoulos, Charles, Philip K. Robins, and Irwin Garfinkel. 1990. "A Structural Model of Labor Supply and Child Care Demand." Discussion paper. Institute for Research on Poverty, University of Wisconsin, Madison, October.

National Association for the Education of Young Children, 1990. *The Early Childhood Advocate* 2, 1 (Fall):1–7.

O'Connell, Martin, and David E. Bloom. 1987. "Juggling Jobs and Babies: America's Child Care Challenge." Publication No. 12. Population Reference Bureau, Washington, DC. February.

Prosser, William R. 1986. "Day Care Centers 1976–1984: Has Supply Kept up with Demand?" Technical Analysis Paper. U.S. Department of Health and Human Services, May.

Robins, Philip K. 1988. "Federal Support for Child Care: Current Policies and a Proposed New System." *Focus* (Institute for Research on Poverty, University of Wisconsin, Madison) 11, 2(Summer):1–9.

————. 1990. "Federal Financing of Child Care: Alternative Approaches and Economic Implications." *Population Research and Policy Review* 9, 1(January):65–90.

U.S. Commission on Civil Rights. 1981. *Child Care and Equal Opportunity for Women.* Clearinghouse Publication No. 67. Washington, DC: U.S. Government Printing Office, June.

U.S. Congress, Congressional Budget Office. 1978. *Childcare and Preschool: Options for Federal Support.* Background paper. Washington, DC: U.S. Government Printing Office, September.

————. 1985. *Reducing Poverty Among Children.* Washington, DC: U.S. Government Printing Office, May.

U.S. Department of Labor. 1988. *"Child Care: A Workforce Issue.* Report of the Secretary's Task Force. Washington, DC, April.

———. Bureau of Labor Statistics. 1989. *Handbook of Labor Statistics.* Bulletin 2340. Washington, DC: U.S. Government Printing Office, August.

U.S. Department of the Treasury, Internal Revenue Service. 1976–1986. *Individual Income Tax Returns.* Publication 1304. Washington, DC: U.S. Government Printing Office.

———. 1989, 1990. *Statistics of Income Bulletin.* Publication 1136. Washington, DC: U.S. Government Printing Office.

U.S. General Accounting Office. 1989. "Child Care: Government Funding Sources, Coordination, and Service Availability." GAO/HRD–90–26BR, October.

Comments on

"Child Care Policy and Research: An Economist's Perspective"

William Prosser

I am honored to comment on this chapter. I have great respect for Dr. Robins—he is one of the first of the few economists who ventured into the field of child care policy analysis. He has been making significant contributions to this field for more than ten years.

In reviewing this chapter, it is useful to make a distinction between policy analysis and advocacy analysis. Child care is a relatively volatile issue involving family, women's rights, and child protection/development issues. Generally the national debate, as evidenced by testimony before the Congress, has been dominated by advocacy analysts.

Policy analysts try to define the problem as precisely as possible, making their objectives and assumptions explicit. They articulate the criteria that they think should be used to evaluate various options, such as economic criteria like equity, efficiency, costs, and economic growth, and other noneconomic criteria, which they believe the decisionmaker will or should use to pick among the various options. They then develop a range of options and use the decision criteria to analyze the pros and cons for each option. They may make recommendations to the decisionmaker giving the reasons for their recommendations, but the final ana-

Mr. Prosser works in the Office of the Assistant Secretary for Planning and Evaluation in the U.S. Department of Health and Human Services (HHS). The opinions expressed in this paper are his and do not necessarily represent HHS policy.

lytical product should be one that makes the best possible case for each option.

Advocacy analysts may follow many of the same analytical techniques as do policy analysts. In the end, however, they will try to make the strongest possible case for their preferred option and minimize the strengths of opposing options. As with a trial lawyer, their ultimate objective is to win the case for their client.

Deliberations in the Congress are generally advocacy-oriented by their very nature. In part, this is because the criteria that might be used to assess various options are the essence of congressional debate. Generally, their deliberations are more value-laden than products of objective science. Thus, testimony by experts is more likely to be dominated by advocacy analysts than by policy analysts. Economists are usually no exception, and their participation in the congressional debate usually bears an advocacy tone. Economists may, however, be more likely to present the pros and cons of various options.

Dr. Robins's paper is an attempt to show how economic analysis is able to add to intelligent debate of the child care issue. He demonstrates how an economic paradigm might be used to shed light on key child care issues such as quality, affordability, and availability. His economic model does better with the more objective issues of affordability and availability than with the more subjective issues surrounding that of child care quality. Economic analysis, as discussed in this paper, generally includes some but not all of the important decision criteria that a complete policy analysis should consider.

COMMENTS

Descriptive Materials

The first half of the paper is basically descriptive, summarizing materials from his earlier writings. He touches on labor force trends and existing federal and state practices—numbers of child care programs, federal/state expenditures, trends in subsidies to consumers and suppliers of child care, and some new data on state tax expenditures. In two brief paragraphs he mentions regulation of child care. The final sections of the descriptive first half discuss current proposals for federal child care legislation and the key policy issues as he sees them.

He summarizes very useful descriptive materials. His data

conform with my understanding of national child care data. I offer, however, the following observations:

- In Figure 2 he presents data on the composition of the labor force, distinguishing between the workers who have children under 18 years of age and those with no child so young. These data are concerned with custodial responsibility, that is, with workers who have children living with them. Divorced or separated fathers, for example, are counted as having no children unless they had reacquired children in their current household, through remarriage or some other means. Although I agree with Dr. Robins that this picture does provide a useful insight into why many employers do not become more concerned about employee child care problems, the picture might be more "fair" if he viewed the issue more dynamically and adjusted for the probabilities of having a child in the future (and remaining with the firm). That analysis requires data much more complicated and, to my knowledge, not readily available.

- Dr. Robins's discussion of why the government should subsidize child care is an example of advocacy analysis rather than of policy analysis. Policy analysis would present the economic arguments (or propositions) both for and against subsidies as cost effective ways to remove barriers to employment and to help parents avoid buying inferior goods/services. For example, availability of child care is a necessary condition for mothers with children to work, but does not guarantee that a mother who wants to work will be able to do so. The proportion of women who are prevented from working in the labor force solely because of a lack of child care is an empirical question. The literature on labor force participation of women could be mentioned, or the discussion at the end of the paper could refer back to this question. The reference to the Family Support Act is somewhat misleading. Its child care subsidy is conditioned upon the mother's being in the AFDC and JOBS programs and being engaged in some type of self-sufficiency activity. The discussion should allude to the equity issues of those mothers in similar conditions but who are not eligible for the subsidies, and what the costs of their subsidies, if equity prevailed, would do to the cost-benefit equations.

- The discussion about trends in federal spending omits exploration of and expenditure data for the Earned Income Tax Credit (EITC). In some respects, this is a logical omission. This tax expenditure is not contingent upon child care, although it is contingent on a family's having at least one worker and at least one child. On the other hand, conservatives have changed the terms of the debate somewhat since they began arguing that child care by a parent should receive as much consideration for federal child care tax expenditures as should child care providers—parental surrogates—who are paid so parents can work. They have raised this as an equity rather than a work expense issue. In 1990, proposed changes to the EITC and the "children's allowance" proposed by President Bush were part of the child care legislative debate.

The economic model of family behavior presented later in the chapter seems to imply the same point. Parents make trade-offs: having one parent stay outside the labor market to provide child care, or having the parent work (and be counted) in the labor market, obtaining market or nonmarket child care.

This new aspect to the debate does not diminish Dr. Robins's picture of the historical trends in federal expenditures toward demand-side rather than supply-side funding. It might, however, modify somewhat the inferences relating to the proportion of funds going to lower-income families, since the EITC is targeted on relatively low-income families with children.

Admittedly, many people would find fault with the inclusion of the EITC costs. However, acknowledgment of the issue would improve the deliberation.

Furthermore, passage of the Family Support Act in 1988 and the 1990 child care legislation will change the trends in both subsidy type and the proportion going to low-income families. Referring to these probable future trends would be helpful for the reader.

• The materials on state programs are the most comprehensive that have appeared. They are a valuable contribution to the literature, particularly the compilation of state child care tax subsidies (Table 3). I have attempted over the last several years to perform some calculations of state tax expenditures, and my estimates are of the same order of magnitude as Dr. Robins's. His work is, however, much more thorough and complete.

• There are just so many topics an author can present in a discussion of this kind. However, if the purpose of the chapter is to help noneconomists understand how economic theory and analytical frameworks can shed light on child care issues, more attention should be given to how economists think about child care regulations (see the chapter by Walker for a discussion of the regulations). There is a vast literature on the effect of government regulations on consumer markets. I spent five years during the late 1970s looking at the issue of the appropriateness of federal day care regulations, and I can say unequivocally that economists can contribute much to the debate about regulating child care, in general, and federal regulations, in particular. I wish that Dr. Robins would add his considerable expertise about child care and economics to sharpen and clarify the current debate about federal child care regulations.

A Structural Model

As a bridge between the descriptive materials and discussion of his structural model, he explores the child care proposals and policy issues that the U.S. Congress debated last year. He uses the key issues to set the stage for his model-building and to indicate what contributions such models can make to informing the public debate.

In the second half of the chapter he sketches a structural model linking consumption of child care, other goods, and leisure. Child care consumption is composed of care provided by parents and others. The model approaches the issue from the point of view of the parent consumer. Unfortunately, the model is silent about supply issues like child care worker salaries. The model discussion is both the most exciting and the most disappointing part of the chapter. There are glimmers of new very creative/provocative work. On the one hand, for the economist, there is not enough to determine what Robins has done and how he did it. On the other hand, for the noneconomist, there is not enough to provide the insights, which I think are there, as to how one might think about child care consumption.

I believe that one of the keys to Robins's approach is the treatment of child care *quality*. His measure of quality will not be sufficient or pleasing to developmental psychologists who would want to relate quality of child care to what happens to the children in child care. However, ten years ago, Dr. Robins equated child care quality to the mothers' educational levels. (The more educated the mother, the higher the quality of care the child was assumed to be receiving). In his model, he uses expenditure on child care as a surrogate for quality—the higher the expenditure on child care at a given price, the higher the quality. The model is based on families maximizing the utility (happiness) they derive from child care quality, other consumption goods, and amounts of work and leisure time, given time and income budget constraints. Parents' wage rates, family nonwage income, demographic variables, and price of child care all are components critical to the mix. (It is not clear how the model handles child care where no money changes hands—which is somewhere between one-third and one-half of child care arrangements.)

Given the model, he can simulate various policy options, like the refundable tax credit, to see what the labor supply response of low-income women might be. The major contribution of the model is that it allows labor supply to respond to changes in the budget constraint caused by changes in government policy. Current simulation models are static and less sophisticated in design. I look forward to reading more about the model and its results.

In his discussion about using models to simulate the effects of different policy options, he considers several dependent care tax-credit alternatives—making the credit refundable, increasing the maximum allowable child care expenses per child per family, and making the credit rate more progressive for low-income families. He states that he believes his proposal "would better satisfy . . . the most important objectives of a national child care policy." I believe that explicit discussion of potential national objectives is a useful contribution.

Dr. Robins concludes by saying "The power of economic analysis is that it can evaluate alternative policies . . . and . . . contribute to the efficient allocation of public resources." I would add, and contribute to the public debate about important social issues. Economic Modeling/Policy Analysis can serve to reduce the rhetoric.

Several examples mentioned by Dr. Robins reveal where his analyses might inform current debates:

- The first example should give pause to some conservatives who are reluctant to finance child care publicly. His model leads to the conclusion that parents may purchase child care that is of low quality even relative to their own standards. Public child care subsidies may lead them to buy better care.

- The second example may give pause to some child care advocates who argue that there has been a great increase in demand for child care that, in turn, has caused shortages in child care. These shortages, they argue, keep many low-income mothers out of the labor force. Sandra Hofferth has shown that the price of child care has remained relatively constant over the last ten to fifteen years. If there were a child care shortage, prices should have gone up. Therefore, this evidence may indicate that the market is operating efficiently and that there is no apparent, significant shortage. However, as Fred Glantz of Abt

Associates, Inc., observes, this line of reasoning assumes that child care quality has remained constant. If quality has deteriorated over time, then the evidence against a supply shortage may be seriously weakened. (Since Dr. Robins assumes that quality is proportional to costs, his analysis cannot speak to Dr. Glantz's argument.)

Given that Dr. Robins says that the major policy issues center around the notions of quality, availability, and affordability, I wish that this discussion or his future work would speak to what Gwen Morgan describes as the Trilema of Center Child Care:

> If as a Nation we have appropriate child-to-staff ratios and teacher qualifications to assure acceptable child safety development, and pay the caregivers reasonable wages (e.g., comparable to school teachers), then the price is beyond what parents are willing to pay. This brings the supply side into the equation not just the demand side analyzed by Dr. Robins.

> Many advocates argue that the pay for child care workers is scandalous. We must have federal programs to raise wages in order to cut down burnout and turnover and to keep the better people in the profession. On the other hand, I do not know how the government can raise child care wages without, for example, taking over the child care industry and operating it like the schools. I am sure that many people would be troubled by such an idea. Economists might analyze this proposition.

3

Public Policy and the Supply of Child Care Services

James R. Walker

There is almost a complete absence of reliable statistical evidence on the operation of the child care market, yet one encounters a (seemingly) infinite supply of personal experiences when discussing child care. This and the emotive nature of children's issues make policy discussions on child care spirited if unconstrained by objective evidence. A common perception held by many users and experts is that the child care market functions poorly. This paper evaluates this perception in light of recent evidence on the child care market and particularly on the supply of child care services.

To make this evaluation, I link the informal notion of a poorly functioning market with the formal, precise concept of imperfect markets developed by economists. In the technical language of economists, perfect markets are fully efficient (the ability to produce the most goods and services for the resources available) and exhibit "an absence of regret"—no individual can be made better off without making another individual worse off. Imperfect markets are inefficient and do not possess the desirable "absence of regret" property. Idealized, perfect markets exist only under very restrictive conditions. Failure of these conditions produces market imperfection (sometimes called market failure). By this view, to state that the child care market functions poorly is equivalent to stating that at least one of the conditions required for market perfection is violated. This paper considers the application of these conditions to the child care market.

A complete evaluation of market performance considers efficiency and equity (the distribution of the goods and services to individuals). This chapter focuses exclusively on the efficiency of the child care market. This focus is adopted for two reasons. First, economics is most insightful on efficiency issues (i.e., the allocation of scarce resources). Moreover, market efficiency is an objective goal, with widespread support, that lends itself to dispassionate consideration. Second, because they are not fully efficient, imperfect markets invite political intervention. A systematic review of the sources of market imperfection is, simultaneously, a systematic review of potential targets of government policy. Moreover, many market imperfections cause distributional inequities. Ignorance of the operation of the market inhibits (arguably prohibits) developing effective redistributional programs. Understanding market operation (or, equivalently, assessing market efficiency) precedes normative policy analysis and design. By concentrating on market efficiency, the present discussion clarifies the motivation for government intervention in the child care market.

CHILD CARE USAGE:
RECENT TRENDS AND POLICY ISSUES

The best recent summary on the general trends of supply and demand for child care in the United States is by Hofferth and Phillips (1987). The most notable of these trends is the increased labor force attachment of women with children. (See also Hayghe 1986.) From 1970 through 1985 the labor force participation rate of married women with children under the age of three doubled so that in 1985, approximately 51 percent of these women participated in the labor market. The Census Bureau predicts the trend will not abate. This rapid growth rate is only one factor responsible for returning child care to a place of prominence on the policy agenda.[1]

Hofferth and Phillips also document that, from 1970 through 1985, the use of relative care declined while market care (by centers and by family home providers) increased. Current usage statistics reveal that, for working mothers with preschool children, about one-half of all child care is provided by relatives, a

---

[1] Another contributing factor is the 1988 Family Support Act, which requires women with children ages 3 and older to work, train, or enroll in school to retain eligibility for AFDC benefits.

quarter by centers and preschools, and the remaining quarter by family home providers. Furthermore, the mode of care used varies with the age of the child. Centers provide care mostly for preschoolers; family home providers extend care to all ages and supply most of the market care for infants.

Information on prices in the child care market is scarce; however, a few patterns emerge. For instance, the hourly cost is low. Estimates range from $1.35 to $2.50 for center care and from $1.00 to $1.30 for family home providers (see Hofferth 1988; Kisker et al. 1989; and Blau forthcoming), putting the weekly cost of full-time child care between $40 and $100. Moreover, recent work by Blau (forthcoming) and Hofferth (1988) reveals that from 1976 through 1985, real weekly household expenditures for child care services remained virtually constant. Not surprisingly, real wages and salaries of child care workers were also low (Blau forthcoming). In fact, wage levels near the minimum are not unusual in this sector.[2] Moreover, returns to education and experience in the industry appear to be minimal (Riley and Rodgers 1989, and Walker 1990).

Juxtaposed against the recent trends in child care usage and expenditures is the perception that the child care market does not function well. Such is the concern of David Edie, forcibly expressed in a recent paper (1989):

> Low and moderate income families simply cannot afford what it costs to have quality services with reasonably paid workers. This dysfunctional supply and demand system frequently results in inadequate supply, mediocre to poor care and poor wages and high turnover.

Others have noted that the inadequacy of supply is seen in the lack of infant care, evening and weekend care, and care of children with special needs (Hofferth and Phillips 1987; Kahn and Kammerman 1987; Brush 1987; Kisker et al. 1989). The market seems unable to generate the full array of care that consumers demand.

In trying to meet the rapid increase in the demand for services, many fear the child care industry has been forced to compromise

---

[2] Using a recent survey of day care establishments in Wisconsin, Riley and Rodgers (1989) estimated that the average starting hourly wage for an assistant teacher (the entry-level position) at a day care center was $3.94; the average hourly wage for an assistant teacher was $4.12; teachers (individuals with full responsibility for children) averaged about $5.00 per hour.

the quality of care it currently offers. The absence of government regulations that enforce minimum care standards intensifies this fear. While all states regulate center care and forty-eight states regulate family home providers, agency budgets are small, supporting limited enforcement staffs.[3] Moreover, because family home providers caring for fewer than a prescribed number of children are exempt from regulation in many states, between only 5 and 10 percent are licensed or certified.[4] Child-development experts note that quality care also results from stable child-provider relationships, but high turnover rates among low-paid workers may make such relationships rare (Floge 1985).

Unfortunately, the trends just presented yield no direct information on the functioning of the child care market. They can indicate either a competitive or an imperfect market. To demonstrate, consider the constant, real weekly expenditures on child care discussed above. Expenditure, of course, is the product of two terms, the price per unit of the good and the number of units purchased (quantity). These terms reflect, implicitly or explicitly, a given level of quality (e.g., "grade-A" eggs). Expenditures will be constant if the price, quantity, and quality are constant over time. If quantity and quality are constant, then constant expenditures imply that prices are also constant. Similarly, if prices and quality are constant in the presence of a large increase in demand, this too indicates that the market is functioning well: supply is sufficiently forthcoming to meet the increasing demand. However, increased demand may open the market to low quality providers. Per-unit prices will then decline in response to the decreased quality of care available in the market. In this instance, expenditures are constant but reflect a lower quality of child care by the end of the period. (The real price per unit of quality increased over the reference period.) These two scenarios illustrate that widespread concern over the availability of quality care may be justified even when expenditure patterns are stable.

As this discussion illustrates, market performance is too subtle to be evaluated using only descriptive statistics; also needed are explicit models of household and firm behavior. Hence, eval-

---

[3] According to a recent U.S. Government Accounting Office report (1989), 26 states license family providers, 14 have mandatory registration, 3 have voluntary registration, and 5 regulate only subsidized family providers.

[4] The prescribed minimums vary considerably: family home providers caring for three or more children are regulated in 22 states, four or more in 17 states, and five or more in 9 states.

uating how well (or how poorly) the child care market functions requires an interpretative framework. This framework is presented later, where I consider the sources of market failure. In preparation for such a framework, and to provide a perspective on the child care market, I now consider the market's special features.

SPECIAL FEATURES OF THE CHILD CARE MARKET

Implicit in many policy discussions is the assumption that the child care market is unique, or at least substantially different from other markets. Identifying these special features will help frame our discussion of the policy instruments available to the government that, if employed, would affect the child care market. In the following two subsections, I discuss the specific features that make the child care market unique. These include the multidimensional aspect of the service and the relatively low cost of entry, particularly in the family home sector. A third subsection presents some descriptive evidence on these issues.

The Multidimensional Nature of Child Care Services

An obvious yet extremely important feature is that child care services possess many dimensions such as price, convenience, reliability, availability, and quality, to mention only a few. These dimensions include characteristics of the child, the provider, and the service; services are identical only if all the attributes or dimensions describing the care are identical. Child care arrangements that differ in convenience, reliability, safety, flexibility, learning opportunity, or nurturing are different services. Children of different ages have different developmental needs that require different mixtures of care attributes. Consequently, the services provided in the care of children of different ages are distinct—infant care is a different service from after-school care or toddler care. Unlike the standard homogeneous "good" of economic textbooks, child care services are heterogeneous.

This product differentiation has two implications for understanding the market. First, because child care services vary on so many dimensions, consumers may trade off various attributes in making their decision. Some consumers, for example, may be willing (at the offered price) to tolerate lower convenience in exchange for greater flexibility; others may be more concerned about a service's reliability than its flexibility; still others may place a higher value on an excellent health and safety record than on a reputation for reliability. The price of child care depends in part upon how consumers value the different attributes of care: prices are determined by both the intensity of consumers' preferences and the number of consumers with identical preferences. Hence, forms of care that are seen as more similar should be better substitutes and should, other factors being equal, sell at more similar prices than do less similar services. If two services are not identical they need not sell at the same price. Even if the child care market is perfectly competitive the market will experience price dispersion.[5]

An important aspect of this economic framework is that child care "quality" is only one of the many dimensions of child care. As a shorthand device when considering heterogeneous products, economists typically collapse the multiple attributes of a product under the single label, "quality." (The discussion of the constant expenditures above is an example.) Though convenient for purposes of analysis and a useful expositional device, such a practice unfortunately presents an oversimplified view of the consumer's decision problem. The use of different terminology, such as "child care services" instead of "quality," recognizes the wider aspect of choice implicit in the economist's perspective and will clarify and facilitate discussions between economists and professionals from other fields. (As noted by Blau in this volume, economists and developmental psychologists currently use "quality" for two different concepts.)

The second implication that product differentiation has for understanding the child care market is that it justifies the diversity of modes currently observed in the market. Different attributes of care may be supplied most effectively by different types of providers. For example, in-home maternal care is one mode, in-home nonrelative care is another, as is the care provided by a family day home or a center. Although each mode offers every attribute of care to some degree, one mode can offer a particular attribute more efficiently (least costly) than the others can. For example, a child's cognitive skills may be developed most efficiently by a mother at home, whereas a child's social skills may be developed most efficiently at a center. These cost advantages in the provision of care lead to specialization and diversity ob-

---

[5]As noted above, price and expenditure are distinct concepts. This discussion refers to price.

served in today's market. As in other industries, cost advantages are a primary determinant of firm behavior. Unfortunately, knowledge of these relationships, although important, is virtually nonexistent for the child care industry.[6]

The Supply of Child Care Services

An important feature of any industry is the ability of new suppliers to enter. Industries with fewer entry and exit barriers generally have larger responses of quantity supplied to changes in price (supply elasticities) because an increase in price stimulates additional output from existing producers and induces new suppliers to enter. Since capital requirements and regulations are entry barriers, and since family providers face lower capital and regulatory requirements, the supply elasticity of family providers should be greater than that for centers, and greater for unregulated providers than for regulated ones.

Supply elasticities are useful because they summarize information on behavioral responses to changes in market conditions. Since there are different supply elasticities for different modes of child care, policies that affect the price of care will change the proportion of suppliers of different types of care and the attributes of care offered in the market.

Although the preceding discussion makes the usual distinction between households and firms, it is noteworthy that this distinction is somewhat blurred in the child care market: unlike the situation in most markets, consumers and producers are not always distinct. Women can act either as net consumers or net producers (Connelly 1988). As the price of child care increases and the net gain from working declines, women can leave their jobs to care for their children at home. In turn, this shift to parental care puts downward pressure on the price of care (consumers have access to good alternatives). But although there is some evidence that family home providers tend to be women with young children (Hofferth and Phillips 1987), Blau (forthcoming) estimates that the child care industry (including family providers) employs only about 1 percent of the female work force. Apparently, paid child care is a service few women decide to offer.

Reasons for this choice are fairly obvious. Caring for other children reduces the time available to spend alone with one's

[6] Mukerjee, Witte, and Hollowell (1990) is an initial study in this area.

own child, and a mother may not want to sacrifice that time, especially for the low wage family providers earn. Moreover, many women simply lack the time (especially when their children are very young) and perhaps the special entrepreneurial skills necessary to run a small business. Finally, a family home provider makes so little money caring for a few children that, absent other sources of income, she cannot afford to take such a job.

Some Evidence on the Family Home Care Market

Family home providers play roles as both consumers and producers and exhibit features of both. As producers, they maximize profits, whereas as consumers they maximize utility (which may not yield maximum profits). But is one role played to the exclusion of the other? Data collected from the Child Care Supply and Needs Survey fielded in 1988 by Mathematica Policy Research for the U.S. Department of Health and Human Services helps answer this question (see Tables 1 and 2). The markets covered were in Newark, New Jersey, and Camden, New Jersey, and South Chicago, Illinois. This survey is one of the few sources of information on the characteristics of the family providers and the care they offer.[7]

Summary statistics on several characteristics are presented in Table 1. Table 2 summarizes the educational attainment of family providers (Panel A), and offers a comparison with local educational attainment levels reported in the 1980 census (Panel B).

Before reviewing Tables 1 and 2, it is important to note that at the time of the survey, the regulatory environments differed in New Jersey and Illinois. Family providers in Illinois caring for four or more children were required to be licensed; in New Jersey, family providers could voluntarily register with the state. Consistent with national estimates, approximately 7 percent of all family providers in South Chicago were licensed. Because of the newness of the program, less than 5 percent were registered in New Jersey.

Panel A of Table 1 reports the number of children under care per establishment (i.e., all children excluding the provider's own). Regulated providers, not surprisingly, care for more children on average. Differences in the average number of children

---

[7] An interesting feature of the survey is that both sides of the child care market are covered. For a detailed discussion of the survey, see Kisker et al. (1989).

TABLE 1

Measures of Establishment Size, Child–Staff Ratios, Experience,
Child Care Earnings, and Commitment to the Profession
for Family Providers in Newark, NJ, Camden, NJ,
and South Chicago, IL

Panel A
Number of Children per Establishment

Statistic	Newark	Camden	South Chicago Unlicensed	South Chicago Licensed
Mean	1.98	2.32	1.99	5.66
Standard Deviation	1.01	1.88	1.31	2.45
Number of Providers	85	119	106	144
Percentage of Providers with:				
1 child	35.0	46.6	47.9	1.1
4 or more children	8.0	16.6	14.9	70.9
8 or more children	0.2	3.0	0.0	5.0

Panel B
Ratio of Child Hours to Provider Hours

Statistic	Newark	Camden	South Chicago Unlicensed	South Chicago Licensed
Mean	1.77	1.47	1.66	3.09
Standard Deviation	.83	.75	.92	1.07
First Quartile	1.00	1.00	2.16	1.00
Median	1.89	1.26	1.50	3.00
Third Quartile	2.00	2.00	4.75	2.01
Interquartile Range	1.01	1.00	1.00	2.59

Panel C
Years of Experience

Statistic	Newark	Camden	South Chicago Unlicensed	South Chicago Licensed
Mean	7.3	6.6	5.3	10.2
Standard Deviation	8.2	8.3	7.0	9.8
First Quartile	1.8	1.0	1.4	2.5
Median	4.0	3.0	3.0	8.0
Third Quartile	10.0	10.0	5.0	15.0
Interquartile Range	8.2	9.0	3.6	12.5

TABLE 1 (*continued*)

Panel D
Annual Gross Earnings from Child Care
(in units of $1000)

Statistic	Newark	Camden	South Chicago Unlicensed	South Chicago Licensed
Mean	3.3	3.9	4.1	9.9
Standard Deviation	3.7	4.6	5.8	5.5
First Quartile	0.6	1.1	1.0	6.1
Median	2.1	2.2	2.4	9.7
Third Quartile	5.0	5.1	4.7	13.6
Interquartile Range	3.4	4.1	3.7	7.7

Panel E
Commitment to the Profession
Percent Responding Yes

Statistic	Newark	Camden	South Chicago Unlicensed	South Chicago Licensed
Member of Family Care Association	0.0	3.2	0.0	42.1
Wants to Be in a Directory	57.5	33.2	27.4	68.6

SOURCE: The Child Care Supply and Needs Survey (1988).

NOTES: In Panel B, children of all ages are included in the numerator of the ratio. Provider hours include the hours of all individuals reported as helping with the care of children. In Panel D, annual gross earnings from child care is defined as (weekly revenue minus cash payments to helpers) times (number of weeks/years of care).

under care per establishment among unregulated providers (in Newark, Camden, and South Chicago) are small. The unregulated providers care for about two children on average; in fact, one-third to almost one-half care for only one child. Unregulated providers appear to offer a form of care that is intensive in the time of the provider.

The statistics on child-to-staff ratios reported in Panel B of Table 1 support this view. (A provider having no helpers and caring for one child will have a ratio of one.) Unregulated providers care for only about half as many children per hour as do licensed providers.

Summary statistics on years of experience are reported in Panel C of Table 1, and educational attainment is reported in Table 2. Experience and education are offered as (perhaps crude)

TABLE 2
Frequency Distribution of Educational Attainment

Panel A
Family Providers in Newark, NJ, Camden, NJ, and South Chicago, IL

Education Level	Newark	Camden	South Chicago Unlicensed	South Chicago Licensed
Less than High School	47.1%	42.9%	29.0%	19.4%
High School Graduate	31.8	24.1	39.0	37.5
Some College	20.0	31.3	30.0	42.4
Post College	1.2	1.8	2.0	0.7
Courses in Child Development	25.9	33.0	35.0	63.2
Special Training in Child Development	23.5	29.0	20.0	56.9

Panel B
Persons 18 Years and Older
(1980 Census)

Education Level	Newark	Camden	South Chicago
Less than High School	41.5%	34.8%	30.9%
High School Graduate	35.3	37.9	37.8
Some College	13.0	14.3	18.8
College Degree	5.9	7.9	7.3
Post College	4.2	5.0	5.2

SOURCES: Panel A: The Child Care Supply and Needs Survey. Panel B: Bureau of the Census, Public Use tapes, 1980 census.

NOTES: Percentages in Panel A are from The Child Care Supply and Needs Survey (1988). Years of schooling reported in Panel B are weighted by the sampling frequency of the zip codes appearing in The Child Care Supply and Needs Survey (1988).

measures of the quality of labor input. Licensed providers have a distinct advantage: they have twice the experience of unregulated providers on average (as measured by the median), are less likely to have dropped out of high school, and are slightly more likely to have some college experience. (The proportion of high school dropouts [the national average is roughly 10 percent], especially among unregulated family providers, is indeed disturbing.) In addition, licensed providers are twice as likely to have had special training or courses in child development.[8] Re-

---

[8] Unlike other states, licensure in Illinois requires no minimum standards for education or training. Family providers must only be at least 18 years of age and of "good moral character." Almost all the regulations apply to the facilities, not the family providers themselves.

call, however, that the Child Care Supply and Needs Survey covered only metropolitan areas. To adjust for the composition of the sample, Panel B of Table 2 reports the educational attainment from the 1980 census for these areas weighted by zip code to match the sample composition of the survey. A comparison of Panels A and B suggests that the educational attainment of family providers still generally reflects the educational patterns in their neighborhoods.

Panel D of Table 1 reports gross earnings of family providers. Only wages paid to helpers have been deducted, the other expenses connected with providing services have not, and consequently the figures in Panel D overestimate earnings. Nevertheless, the mean and median reported in Panel D are consistent with the low wages child care workers earn, as discussed earlier. Licensed providers make two to three times the annual earnings of unlicensed providers. In fact, earnings in the first quartile for licensed providers exceed the third quartile earnings of unregulated providers. This earnings distribution is consistent with the distribution of children under care reported in Panel B. The difference between licensed and unlicensed providers is most evident in terms of income: licensed providers earn little; unlicensed providers earn even less.

Finally, Panel E of Table 1 presents some evidence on degrees of attachment to the profession. The first row reports the percentage of family providers who are members of the Family Care Association. (Membership in this association is considered to indicate a level of commitment to the profession.) Practically speaking, only licensed providers are members; in fact, *none* of the unregulated providers in Newark or South Chicago is a member. The second row reports the percentage of each group willing to be listed in a child care directory (another sign of commitment). Although the difference between licensed and unlicensed providers is not so striking here, licensed providers still show a greater willingness to be listed (compare the responses in Chicago). Experience within the profession is yet another measure of attachment. The greater experience levels of licensed family providers reported in Panel C are consistent with the responses in Panel E.

To answer the question "What is the correct characterization of the behavior of family providers?" my interpretation of the patterns reported in Tables 1 and 2 is that both pure types exist. And, for policy purposes, the categories can be distinguished by their regulatory status: licensed family providers appear to be "profit maximizers" while unlicensed providers appear to be "utility maximizers," not interested in maximizing their income from child care.

The substantial heterogeneity of family providers has two important policy implications. First, regulated family providers are not representative of all family home providers: therefore, inferences drawn from samples of only regulated providers will be biased. For example, because they already (or more closely) adhere to existing regulations, it may be less costly for licensed family providers to satisfy additional, more stringent regulations. For this group, compliance rates may be high and exit rates, induced by the regulations, low. Similarly, for unregulated providers, the cost of meeting new regulations (if enforced) may be prohibitive; unlicensed providers will either cease providing services or go (deeper) underground to avoid detection. Again, although regulated providers are easier to sample, inference drawn from such highly selective samples will be misleading; therefore, samples must include regulated and unregulated providers.

Second, the low earnings of family providers in general, and their implied preference for child care as an item of consumption ("utility maximization") rather than a source of income, seriously limit the ability of unregulated providers to make investments that would improve the quality of the care they provide. Minimum standards (e.g., stricter building requirements) impose a cost on providers and may, as discussed above, severely affect supply (withdrawal) or compliance (evasion). Regulatory policy must therefore operate on a razor's edge.

These differences between providers and the wide variety of services available in the market make the coordination of buyers and sellers complex. Any analysis of the child care market entails an analysis of several distinct but related services. A coordination problem in any of these services may perpetuate the perception that "the child care market does not work well." In the next pages I review this and other sources of market imperfection.

SOURCES OF MARKET IMPERFECTION

To study market imperfections, it is useful to have the concept of a perfect market as a reference point. Our guide is the first law of welfare economics: that if firms and households act competitively as price-takers (i.e., not monopolists), and have complete information, and if a full set of markets exists, then the market will be efficient (Atkinson and Stiglitz 1980, p. 343). That is, the market will tend toward an equilibrium in which no one can be made better off without making someone else worse off. This is the standard efficiency result of competitive markets and is a formal statement of Adam Smith's invisible hand. Market imperfection occurs when one or more of these conditions are violated. Although boundaries between causes of market imperfection are blurred (a violation of one condition produces violations of the other), the conditions of the theorem provide a useful framework for reviewing possible forms of imperfection in the child care market.

In identifying a market imperfection, one identifies a potential target of government intervention, and not, contrary to what is said in the child care advocacy literature, a mandate for it. The latter requires additional evidence that intervention will be effective. In the presence of a market imperfection, support for government intervention requires some evidence that the government can avoid the problems that induced the imperfection in the first place. In the following discussion I highlight two areas in which government intervention may not be effective.

Noncompetitive Behavior

Noncompetitive behavior traditionally results when a firm or household is no longer "small" in comparison with the market and its actions affect the market price (market power). Classic examples are monopolies (one seller) and monopsonies (one buyer). Competitive firms have no market power and must take the market price as given; any attempt to charge more results in the loss of all customers (consumers know plenty of identical firms willing to sell the product at the market price). But when the market structure is characterized by product differentiation and a large number of firms, all with some market power, the result is known as monopolistic competition. Issues normally associated with monopolistic competition are inefficient production and brand proliferation. Inefficient production occurs when firms act like monopolies and set prices above marginal cost; brand proliferation occurs as firms seek to carve separate niches in the marketplace. The welfare cost to society of these noncompetitive acts depends on the exact structure of the market (Tirole

1988, p. 288). Generally, however, as the number of firms increases, welfare costs of monopolistic competition decrease. Returning to the child care market, since home production is another form of care, the inefficiency introduced by monopolistic competition is small (there are a large number of potential providers). Viewing the child care industry as monopolistically competitive raises a question as to the source of the market power of providers. In the next section, I argue that child care providers have market power because of imperfect information.

Imperfect Information

The lack of perfect information is the most striking difference between the child care market and the idealized perfect market. There are two reasons that imperfect information exists. First, unlike the consumers described in economic textbooks, child care users do not know the identity of every potential supplier. Information is obtained informally and consumers must actively search to find a provider. Second, consumers do not know the quality of care offered by providers once identified. Even after a long period of use, consumers will not be fully informed about the behavior of the provider. Both forms of uncertainty have important implications for market performance.

An important aspect of the child care industry is the informal way in which information is obtained about providers. According to the responses recorded in Table 3, approximately 75 percent of all users either know their provider personally beforehand or are referred via friends, neighbors, or relatives. More formal sources, such as newspapers and referrals by community agencies and caseworkers, are less widely used. These results suggest that once informal leads are exhausted, consumers may have limited information to help them locate adequate child care.

Consumer awareness of the amount of time and effort required to find an adequate provider perpetuates the notion that the "child care market does not function well." The willingness of consumers to search for a family provider depends on the expected ease of finding one, as well as the availability and characteristics of alternative forms of care. Women with partners or relatives available to help with care are less likely to search, as are women with strong preferences to stay home and care for their own children. Consequently, women with limited access to market care and women with good alternatives to market care

TABLE 3

How Users First Learned of Providers

| | Newark | | Camden | | South Chicago | |
	Center	Family Provider	Center	Family Provider	Center	Family Provider
Referrals from Friends/ Neighbors/Relatives	66.5%	57.7%	53.2%	45.9%	52.7%	55.4%
Already Knew Provider	14.5	27.8	7.0	28.5	21.6	18.6
Newspapers and Advertisements	7.8	6.6	20.3	15.1	6.3	14.6
Referrals from Community Agency (not caseworker)	3.3	2.7	2.7	2.1	4.1	6.2
Referrals from Caseworker	0.0	0.0	5.7	1.4	2.3	0.9
Cared for Older Child	0.0	0.0	3.6	0.0	0.3	0.0
Other	7.9	5.2	7.5	7.0	13.7	4.3

SOURCE: The Child Care Supply and Needs Survey (1988).

may both report that a long time was needed to find "adequate" market care. An important task for future research will be to distinguish between these two groups of women.

To lower search costs, policymakers frequently recommend programs to fund resource and referral agencies that help match users and providers. The success of these programs hinges on their ability to maintain comprehensive and accurate lists of providers in each neighborhood. The responses reported in Table 4 suggest that unregulated family providers are quite passive in seeking clients. More than half of the unregulated family providers report taking no steps to find clients. Consistent with the results presented in Table 3, most providers make contact with users through referrals from friends, neighbors, and relatives. A comparison of the actions taken by licensed and unregulated providers suggests that the latter are unwilling to reveal their identity to third parties. (Most striking in this regard is the difference between licensed and unlicensed providers in South Chicago.) This unwillingness works against resource and referral programs. The small size of the groups taken care of by most family providers and the informal manner in which information is obtained also work against detection. Furthermore, high turnover rates among unregulated providers make referral lists costly to maintain. In summary, high turnover rates among family providers because of low wages, and the difficulty of identifying those not registered, inhibit any referral program. These considerations suggest that government intervention on behalf of referral programs may not be effective.

TABLE 4

Actions Taken by Family Providers to Find Clients

	Newark	Camden	South Chicago Unlicensed	South Chicago Licensed
No Steps	54.8%	53.3%	56.1%	29.1%
Referrals from Friends, Neighbors, and Relatives	19.4	17.4	16.2	45.7
Newspapers and Advertisements	9.0	17.5	2.7	30.6
Referrals from Community Agency (not caseworker)	0.0	1.2	2.7	22.8
Bulletin Boards	2.5	2.1	2.3	25.8
Talk to Families with Children	2.3	1.2	0.9	8.6
Referrals from Caseworker	1.5	0.2	0.0	5.9

SOURCE: The Child Care Supply and Needs Survey (1988).

NOTES: Some providers may take more than one action to find clients. Column percentages may sum to more than 100.

The second reason that imperfect information exists for all firms (and persists for as long as the child is in care) is that consumers are imperfectly informed about the attributes of care and the effort of the provider, because, as with other services, it is difficult for consumers to monitor the producer. The provider can be interviewed and the facilities inspected, yet the consumer can never be perfectly informed about the care his or her child receives.[9]

A key feature of this imperfection is that consumers know less about the quality of care than do providers. Well studied in the economics literature, this informational problem is separated into two types: adverse selection and hidden action (moral hazard). In models of adverse selection, potential providers have no control over quality, but decide, depending on market conditions, whether to enter the market. Adverse selection occurs if only low quality providers enter the market (high quality providers have better opportunities outside the child care market).[10] Notice that market quality of care is "low" not because providers

---

[9] In his remarks made at "The Economics of Child Care" conference, May 16, 1990, at the University of North Carolina–Chapel Hill, Richard Clifford noted that study teams have observed that centers tend to change children's diapers just prior to pickup by the parents. Also, when questioned by parents on staff shortages, center staff tend to underreport the duration of the (temporary) shortfall.

[10] In these models, the value of the provider's next best opportunity is the relevant cost of quality.

defraud or cheat consumers, but because the average ability of providers entering the industry is "too low." In models of hidden action, providers control their quality of service. Furthermore, it is assumed that higher quality care is more expensive to produce. "Moral hazard" occurs when providers cheat in their provision of quality: they defraud consumers who cannot perfectly monitor them.

Adverse selection and hidden action can occur simultaneously and can affect both family providers and centers. With centers, the potential for adverse selection is perhaps lower than that for providers, while the potential for hidden action is higher. Center care is more closely regulated: their facilities should conform to minimum standards set by the industry, and the members of their staff must have formal child care training. Thus, low quality centers should be few and the potential for adverse selection slight. The day-to-day action of the staff, however, cannot be monitored so easily; therefore, the potential for hidden action is (theoretically) high.

With family home providers, the situation is reversed: the potential for adverse selection is perhaps higher, whereas that for hidden action is lower. Because of the low wages family providers earn, individuals with more marketable skills will seek employment in other fields. Thus, low-skill individuals are most likely to become family providers; the potential for adverse selection is relatively high. However, if a family provider cares for her own child while caring for another's, any malfeasance will jeopardize her own child's welfare; thus, the presence of one's own child guards against shirking. Also, the apparent lack of interest on the part of providers in maximizing income makes it unlikely that they will cheat or mistreat children to save a few dollars.

Leland (1979) considers the problem of adverse selection and Shapiro (1986), problems of hidden action as they both investigate the effects of occupational licensure on the provision of professional services. In the model by Leland, licensure restricts the lowest quality providers from entering the market; thus, average provider quality increases as does market price.[11] Leland

---

[11] Leland's model is an application of the insight of Akerlof's (1970) model on the used car market. Demand for the service depends on its price and the average quality of the service in the market. Market failure occurs because the market rewards average quality while providers seek a return on marginal quality. For higher quality providers, the value of their marginal quality exceeds the average quality in the market. Consequently, the higher quality providers work elsewhere. In the extreme

finds that minimum quality standards will be more advantageous to consumers under the following conditions: (1) the price elasticity of demand is low; (2) demand is sensitive to variation in quality; (3) the marginal cost of providing quality care is low; and (4) consumers place a low value on low quality service. Whether these conditions are met by the child care market (and perhaps most particularly by the market for family provider care) is an empirical issue; nevertheless, two speculative observations are offered. First, since child care can be produced at home, the price elasticity of demand for care may be large (violating condition [1]). Second, the apparent inability of family providers to obtain a return for increased training implies that demand is not sensitive to variations in quality variation (violating condition [2]).

Shapiro's model (1986) recognizes that because of information problems, regulations control inputs and, indirectly, the quality of service, while providers control quality through investments in training. Since occupational licensure establishes minimum educational requirements, individuals with the highest level of training are assumed to produce the highest quality of service. Licensed providers establish a reputation for the provision of high quality care. Any licensed provider caught shirking is deemed (now and forever) to be a low quality provider.

Two predictions emerge from this model. First, licensed providers must receive a premium to cover the cost of training and education. Indeed, the threat of potential loss of this premium dissuades providers from shirking. Second, regulations benefit consumers who value quality more than those who do not, and raise the cost (and the level) of the lowest quality of service available. Individuals who were previously satisfied consuming this lowest quality service must purchase, after regulation, care from "overtrained" professionals at a higher price. No empirical studies of the fee structure of centers exist as of yet that evaluate these predictions.

Two important caveats must be noted here that may negate predictions derived from these models. First, both models assume that quality is unidimensional. Under this assumption it is meaningful to speak of "high" versus "low quality" providers. Such simple categories vanish once quality is permitted to have

---

case, no providers enter and there is complete market failure. In general, the extreme case need not occur, as there will be only some reduced (suboptimal) provision of care.

more than a single dimension. Second, the models assume that care standards are costless to enforce. This is implausible, however, especially in the case of family providers. Since only providers caring for more than a prescribed number of children are regulated, licensure can be avoided by caring for a number of children below that prescribed. Monitoring the remaining providers required to be licensed is certainly not free (nor easy). Indeed, since it is so costly, the provocative question arises: Do government agencies possess an advantage in monitoring compliance? The answer appears to be no. Without the same access to the informal sources of information, and with their limited enforcement staff, government agencies may be less efficient at monitoring compliance than an individual consumer may be.

A license is an indication of high quality service.[12] But a family provider caring for her own child while caring for another's can indicate high quality service, too (the potential for hidden action is low). In fact, this may be a more reliable indicator than licensure or certification. The use of volunteers may lower the potential for hidden action in centers, too, and hence encourage high quality service.[13] Therefore, information problems exist, but it is not certain that licensure is an effective remedy for them. The models of Leland and Shapiro provide useful frameworks but must be modified to be fully applicable to the child care market.

Incomplete Markets

The last source of market imperfection is incomplete markets. Complete markets exist when any individual is able to exchange any good, either directly or indirectly, with any other individual (Wilson 1987, p. 180). Implicit in this definition is that the exchange is possible at some price. For an exchange not to occur, however, does not necessarily indicate incomplete markets; a lack of exchange may mean only that the price consumers are willing to pay for a good is less than the cost of producing it.

Many examples of incomplete markets involve the inability to arrange trades across time periods. (Complete markets require

---

[12] For consumers, the license does not seem to separate high from low quality providers. In South Chicago, only 7 percent to 10 percent of all family providers are licensed, yet over 30 percent of those who use family providers state that their provider is licensed.

[13] To ensure a quality environment for her child, a volunteer will provide quality care to other children. Moreover, efforts to increase volunteer involvement also signal that the care establishment is of a sufficiently high quality to withstand continued parental inspection.

the ability to exchange goods now and in the future.) A classic example, tailored to the child care market, is as follows. Suppose that women will enter the labor force only if center care is available. Furthermore, assume that the construction of child care centers requires substantial investment and planning. Now, if women cannot reveal their future demand for center care, no construction of child care centers will occur. Center care will not be available, and an incomplete market will result. If a futures market for day care slots exists, however, consumers can reveal their demand for future care by paying now for the right to a day care slot in the future period, and the market becomes complete. The existence of incomplete markets depends directly upon current institutional forms, including the establishment of property rights, trading mechanisms, and costs of exchange. The present example illustrates that the absence of complete markets frequently reflects another form of market imperfection.

Another common source of incomplete markets is "externalities." An externality is any action by an individual or firm that directly affects others beyond any effect communicated by the price system (Atkinson and Stiglitz 1980, p. 8). Water pollution is a classic example of a negative externality. The polluting manufacturer, in determining a production plan, considers only the value of the output and not the cost of the pollution on others. Externalities give rise to incomplete markets in the following sense. Expansion in the number of markets, through the assignment of property rights, sometimes solves problems caused by externalities.[14]

Concern over externalities plays a major role in policy discussions of the child care market. To recognize this, view child care as a form of education. Just as underinvestment in education by some households exerts negative effects on others, so would underinvestment in the quality of child care.[15] Issues and problems generated by externalities are important. However, there is little consensus on the appropriate remedies for externalities.[16]

---

[14] Taxes and subsidies represent another solution. Which method is used to correct the externality depends on the viability and enforceability of each. In the water pollution example, the creation of a market for "pollution rights" expands the set of markets and incorporates the pollution externality within the price system (Laffont 1988, p. 14).

[15] See Crawford and Pollak (1990) for an extensive discussion of this and related issues.

[16] However, as in many educational issues, taxes and subsidies are common policy instruments. No one takes seriously a proposal that, in addressing underinvestment in child care quality, defines "child quality rights" as analogous to the "pollution rights" mentioned above.

Incomplete markets need not eliminate all transactions, but do imply that some individuals will be unable to make their desired transactions. Indeed, the most frequent complaint made against centers is of rationing: some consumers who would like to use center care cannot and must queue for care. Of consumers who queue for care, some eventually receive center care, whereas others never do. Queues and waiting lists can indicate rationing and an undersupply (excess demand) of center care. Implicit is that this undersupply is persistent. Yet, as the following discussion reveals, queues can arise for several reasons, of which long-run excess demand due to incomplete markets is only one.

At a fundamental level, services cannot be stored. Queues (waiting lists) are a way to smooth fluctuations in demand. Also, queues can reflect only short-run phenomena. If there are adjustment costs, an otherwise well-functioning market requires time to adjust to changes in the environment. For example, an increased demand for center slots (generated perhaps by increased consumer subsidies) cannot be met immediately; time is required for existing centers to expand and new ones to open. In the short run, queues exist as supply expands. Even though possible, this scenario does not accord with the special features of the child care industry. Low capital requirements and minimal care regulations permit substantial flexibility by potential family providers. The industry is not characterized by the long investment lead times connected with adjustment costs. Moreover, slow supply adjustments to changes in demand should increase prices and wages. Blau's (forthcoming) evidence, cited earlier, indicates that this does not occur. To the extent that queues exist for child care, they are not the result of adjustment costs.

A further analogy to the education industry may be used to support the argument that queues are productive. Colleges and universities use queues (applications), yet few would argue that colleges and universities are in short supply. For a school, queues provide a means by which demand is smoothed and a preferred mix of student attributes is maintained. When application costs are low, gains from acceptance high, and a substantial uncertainty of acceptance exists, a student need not spend much time determining whether a particular school is his/her most preferred school. Rather, the student applies to several schools, waits for acceptance, and then, with knowledge of all the available alternatives, selects a school. For schools and for prospective students, queues are productive.

In this example, apparent demand (the sum of all the waiting lists) far exceeds actual demand (number of individuals seeking acceptance); thus, waiting lists are a poor measure of actual demand. Moreover, knowing the queue discipline—who is served and how waiting lists are processed—is an important datum for evaluating supplier behavior. Child care centers may use queues for the same reasons as do other selective educational institutions.

Child care centers are also similar to colleges in a way that provides another motivation for using queues and waiting lists: many are highly subsidized by private groups or the government, so that fees charged do not reflect the total cost of providing the service. In these circumstances, queues may serve the role of prices that are unable to adjust to the excess demand because of the regulations imposed by the subsidizing agency. In the child care market, for example, many churches subsidize day care centers by renting space at zero or below market rental fees. Volunteer labor can also offset the cost of service, as can government subsidies such as the Child Care Food Program.

Although for-profit and nonprofit organizations can receive subsidies, the work of Weisbrod (1988) suggests that the latter have greater access to subsidies. Assume for the sake of argument that this is true. Also assume (as seems plausible) that, since nonprofit organizations have a greater number of objectives than just profit maximization, the number of slots and the prices charged by nonprofit centers will not be determined by the market. Consequently, a limited number of slots priced below the market can be offered by nonprofit centers. For-profit institutions, facing the same operating costs but with less access to operating subsidies, cannot offer the same price, and therefore must compete on nonprice dimensions. For example, they may offer quicker (if not immediate) access to child care. If true, then prices and queues will be used to allocate the limited number of fixed-price slots. Individuals wanting quicker access to center care will then pay the higher price and use for-profit center care; those who can wait, and those who are most price sensitive, queue for care by applying for a slot at a nonprofit center. In equilibrium, prices and queue lengths balance the demand for, with the supply of, low-cost and high-cost slots.[17]

---

[17] If nonprofit centers are viewed by consumers as offering higher quality care, then the demand for nonprofit slots will be even greater. The equilibrium queue length will be longer, relative to the one described in the text.

FUTURE RESEARCH

The preceding discussion has used the first law of welfare economics to identify several potential sources of imperfection in the child care market. Future research remains to determine whether these imperfections indeed exist. The variety of explanations proposed to rationalize the recent trends of expenditures, wages, and usage in the child care market illustrates how little we know about its operation. What issues seem to be the most pressing? To focus my comments, I limit my answer to three.

1. Unidimensional notions of child care "quality," though conventional and convenient, are misleading. We must recognize the multidimensional nature of child care and define precisely the attributes of care under evaluation. The diversity of suppliers existing in the market can be understood only by recognizing these many dimensions. Such recognition will eliminate simple notions such as "low" and "high" quality providers, while recognizing the many attributes valued by consumers. Since output measures of quality are impossible to define and quantify, I urge economists to adopt an input-based measure of quality, similar to the one in the developmental psychology literature. A focus on inputs naturally leads to studying the process of child care.

2. Knowledge of costs and supply elasticities for each mode of care is needed. Even in competitive markets, knowledge of supply and demand elasticities is required to evaluate the effect of policy changes on market prices (and consumer welfare). Measuring these elasticities requires knowledge of several factors, including entry and exit barriers. Only through this information, in conjunction with studies of demand, can we assess whether policies operate through the demand or supply side of the market.

3. Knowledge of behavioral differences between regulated and unregulated providers is also needed. What is the effect of regulations on the provision and characteristics (especially quality) of the services offered by family providers and on their decision to remain in the unregulated sector? We do not know. Clearly such knowledge is central for designing appropriate regulations. Concerning the behavior of centers, additional studies are needed to determine how the combination of nonprofit and for-profit firms influences market outcomes (e.g., the attributes of care offered or the pricing policies used). Additional studies are also needed to assess whether queues for center care are productive or merely reflect long-run excess demand.

Decisionmakers are forced to act. The proposed research agenda will increase the knowledge required to evaluate the operation of the child care market and how effective government intervention would be. Perhaps the economist's primary contribution to public policy discussions is the recognition and acceptance that policies directly and indirectly affect behavior. The better we understand the behavior of child care consumers and providers the better chance we have of reducing any unintended consequences of interventions in the marketplace. This chapter has presented many conjectures on the behavioral relationships that lie behind the descriptive statistics summarizing our knowledge of the child care market. The fact that many different interpretations are plausible indicates how limited our knowledge currently is; better data and improved behavioral models are needed to determine which interpretation is correct. Therein lies the challenge of future research.

I thank Duncan Chaplin, Ian Gale, William Gormley, James Heckman, Thomas Holmes, Joseph Hotz, Michael Lettau, and Charles Manski for useful discussions. Written comments by Deborah Phillips and David Blau and the editorial assistance of Paul Dudenhefer led to substantial improvements. This research has been supported by a grant from the Department of Health and Human Services to the Institute for Research on Poverty, and by Project HD 19226 from the National Institute of Child Health and Development.

REFERENCES

Akerlof, G. 1970. "The Market for Lemons." *Quarterly Journal of Economics* 84:488–500.

Atkinson, A., and J. Stiglitz. 1980. *Lectures in Public Economics.* New York: McGraw-Hill.

Blau, D. Forthcoming. "The Child Care Labor Market." *Journal of Human Resources,* forthcoming, Winter 1992.

Brush, L. 1987. "Child Care Used by Working Women in the AFDC Population: An Analysis of the SIPP Database." Unpublished manuscript. Working Paper, Office of Social Services Policy, Assistant Secretary for Planning and Evaluation, Department of Health and Human Services, Washington, DC.

Connelly, R. 1988. "The Barriers to Increasing the Supply of Quality

Affordable Child Care." Unpublished manuscript. Brunswick, ME: Bowdoin College.

Crawford, D., and R. Pollak. 1990. "Child Care Policy." Unpublished manuscript. Seattle, WA: University of Washington.

Edie, D. 1989. "Public Policy Crossroads: Child Care and Early Education in Wisconsin." Bureau of Children, Youth and Families, Department of Health and Social Services, Madison, WI.

Floge, L. 1985. "The Dynamics of Child-Care Use and Some Implications for Women's Employment." *Journal of Marriage and the Family* (February):143–154.

Hayghe, H. 1986. "Rise in Mothers' Labor Force Activity Includes Those with Infants." *Monthly Labor Review* (February):43–45.

Hofferth, Sandra. 1988. "The Current Child Care Debate in Context." Unpublished manuscript. Bethesda, MD: National Institute of Child Health and Development.

Hofferth, Sandra, and Deborah A. Phillips. 1987. "Child Care in the United States, 1970 to 1995." *Journal of Marriage and the Family* 49(August):559–571.

Kahn, A., and S. Kammerman. 1987. *Child Care: Facing the Hard Choices.* Dover, MA: Auburn University House Publishing, Inc.

Kisker, Ellen, Rebecca Maynard, Anne Gordon, and Margaret Strain. 1989. "The Child Care Challenge: What Do Parents Need and What Is Available in Three Metropolitan Areas." Report prepared for Department of Health and Human Services by Mathematica Policy Research, Princeton, NJ, February 9.

Laffont, J.-J. 1988. *Fundamentals of Public Economics.* Cambridge, MA: MIT Press.

Leland, H. 1979. "Quacks, Lemons, and Licensing: A Theory of Minimum Quality Standards." *Journal of Political Economy* 87:1328–1346.

Mukerjee, S., A. Witte, and S. Hollowell. 1990. "Provision of Child Care: Cost Functions for Profit-Making and Not-for-Profit Day Care Centers." Working paper #3345. National Bureau of Economic Research, Cambridge, MA.

Riley, D., and K. Rodgers. 1989. "Pay, Benefits and Job Satisfaction of Wisconsin Child Care Providers and Early Education Teachers." Report to the Wisconsin Early Childhood Association, Madison, WI.

Shapiro, C. 1986. "Investment, Moral Hazard, and Occupational Licensing." *Review of Economic Studies* 53:843–862.

Tirole, J. 1988. *The Theory of Industrial Organization.* Cambridge, MA: MIT Press.

U. S. General Accounting Office. 1989. "Child Care: Government Funding Sources, Coordination and Service Availability." GAO/HRD-90-26BR, October.

Walker, J. 1990. "New Evidence on the Supply of Child Care: A Statistical Portrait of Family Providers and an Analysis of Their Fees." Unpublished manuscript. Madison, WI: University of Wisconsin. *Journal of Human Resources*, forthcoming, Winter 1992.

Weisbrod, B. 1988. *The Nonprofit Economy.* Cambridge, MA: Harvard University Press.

Wilson, C. 1987. "Incomplete Markets." In *The New Palgrave: Allocation, Information and Markets*, edited by J. Eatwell, M. Milgate, and P. Newman. New York: W. W. Norton.

≈≈≈≈≈≈≈≈≈≈≈≈≈

Comments on

"Public Policy and the Supply of Child Care Services"
A developmental psychologist's perspective

Deborah A. Phillips

The paper by James Walker focuses on supply issues in child care. He offers us a framework for analyzing the functioning of the child care market based on neoclassical economic notions of market imperfections. He acknowledges that, in most cases, it is a framework not yet filled in with data. But it is extremely useful in disciplining child care researchers to avoid generalized claims that there is a supply crisis in the child care market. Walker cautions that just as child care services are multidimensional—varying in type, quality, price, and reliability, for example—the components of an *effective* child care market are multidimensional. The task that lies before child care researchers is, first, to identify these components and then to decipher where the market is and is not working effectively. It is also commendable that Walker addresses these issues from a stance of skepticism about the applicability of traditional economic assumptions to the child care market. Rather than assume that these assumptions are appropriate for child care, he analyzes their fit to a somewhat atypical market.

My comments have three purposes: First, I will contribute some data to Walker's framework, drawing upon new results from the National Child Care Staffing Study (Whitebook, Howes, and Phillips 1990). Second, I make a few more general comments about Walker's framework, focusing on the three types of market imperfections that he highlights. Third, I suggest the inclusion of equity as an indicator of market success or failure.

NATIONAL CHILD CARE STAFFING STUDY

The National Child Care Staffing Study (Whitebook, Howes, and Phillips 1990), conducted in the spring and summer of 1988, was designed to address four major policy questions:

1. Who teaches in America's child care centers?
2. What do they contribute to the quality of care provided?
3. Do centers that meet or fail to meet nationally established quality guidelines, that operate under different financial and legal auspices, and that serve families from different socioeconomic backgrounds also differ in the quality of care offered to children or the work environments offered to their staff?
4. How have center-based child care services changed from 1977 to 1988?

The study was conducted in five metropolitan areas: Atlanta, Boston, Detroit, Phoenix, and Seattle. The sample consisted of 227 licensed, full-day child care centers, encompassing a representative distribution of nonprofit and for-profit centers, and serving families from all socioeconomic groups. This study can begin to address three specific data needs identified by Walker: price, trends in wages and salaries, and returns to education.

With respect to price, representative center-based care exceeds the $50 weekly cost, presented by Walker, that aggregates family day care and center care. Specifically, full-time infant care averaged $92.36 per week, and varied from $150.96 per week in Boston to $62.01 per week in Atlanta. The average price dropped to $82.01 per week for toddlers and to $70.44 per week for preschoolers. Across the study sites, higher quality centers charged higher prices, as one might expect.

It is now well documented that child care workers earn poverty-level wages. Data concerning trends in child care wages are, however, both less available and less consistent. Walker suggests that wages have remained virtually constant, based on Blau's (1990) analysis of Current Population Survey data from 1976 to 1986 for national random samples of child care workers. In contrast, data from the National Child Care Staffing Study suggest that real wages for center-based child care teachers have dropped by 27 percent and wages for assistant teachers have dropped by 20 percent when compared to 1977 data from the National Day Care Study (Coelen, Glantz, and Calore 1978). Unfortunately, the multiple differences in samples, time frames, and location of employment in these two trend reports make impossible any systematic analysis of the differences. Both reports, however, call attention to the fact that child care wages constitute a major subsidy in the child care market. Blau places his data in the context of increases in child care subsidies between 1976 and 1986 and concludes that these subsidies are not passed on to child care workers in the form of increased wages, thereby containing the costs of child care for parents. We interpret our data to indicate a growing wage subsidization of child care, and also suggest that this trend is driven by concerns about affordability.

These wages do not preclude single and low-income women from the profession, as was also proposed by Walker. Less than half of our sample of child care workers was married, indicating that they did not rely on a second income. Ten percent consisted of single parents living alone with their children, and 22 percent lived alone without children.

With respect to returns on education, they are modest, as Walker speculates. For example, the differential pay between an assistant teacher with only a high school diploma ($4.51) and an assistant teacher with a college degree ($5.32) is $0.81 an hour. For teachers, this differential is $1.79. Even more striking comparisons occur when the earnings of child care workers are compared to the earnings of comparably educated women in the civilian labor force. A working woman with a college degree earns, on average, $26,066 a year for full-time work, compared to the average full-time salary of $11,603 for a child care worker with a college degree. Walker has examined this issue among family day care providers serving low-income families, and similarly reported no returns in the form of higher fees for education and training (Walker 1990).

GENERAL COMMENTS ON WALKER'S FRAMEWORK

Walker's general framework identifies three conditions of market imperfection: noncompetitive behavior, imperfect information, and incomplete markets.

Starting with noncompetitive behavior, it appears that center-based child care providers are acutely sensitive to the market price of child care. Despite significant variation in quality between nonprofit and for-profit centers reported in the National Child Care Staffing Study, there were no differences between nonprofit and for-profit centers in the price of child care within any of the five study sites. This suggests that center providers adjust their prices to what the market can bear. This is possible in the context of wide variation in quality because parents are not particularly well-informed consumers (a sign of imperfect information) and because parents perceive that they have few options when selecting child care (Shinn, Galinsky, and Gulcur 1989) and often report that they were unable to obtain their first choice of arrangements (Sonenstein 1991). Parents, for example, are not able to transport their child to or to pay for *any* available center. These data also suggest that the equating of quality with cost breaks down, to some extent, at the local level.

It is the case, however, that firms have sought to carve separate niches in the marketplace. Specifically, the for-profit chains have explicitly catered to middle-class families and have assiduously avoided locating in low-income neighborhoods. Because households are stratified across neighborhoods by income, and because most parents seek neighborhood-based child care, this niche-building reduces competition and highlights the importance of considering the neighborhood basis of the child care market in economic models. Along these lines, the image of consumers portrayed in portions of Walker's paper as able to "trade off various attributes in making their decision" suggests far greater flexibility than most families have or are willing to act upon.

With respect to imperfect information about the attributes of child care, two interesting questions arise. First, what do we know about how well- or ill-informed parents are about the important attributes of care? Second, do regulations eliminate low quality centers, as Walker suggests? Answers to these questions are directly applicable to Walker's assumption that hidden action better characterizes the information problems of centers while adverse selection is more appropriate for family providers.

The data regarding parent knowledge of the aspects of care that developmental psychologists have found to predict positive child outcomes (see Phillips 1987, and Hayes, Palmer, and Zaslow 1990 for recent reviews of this literature) are complex. Some findings (Hofferth and Wissoker 1990; Shinn, Phillips, Howes, Galinsky, and Whitebook 1990) suggest that parents both pay for and base their satisfaction with child care on the attributes of centers, such as ratios and turnover rates, that have received empirical support as the key ingredients of child care quality. Other investigators (Sonenstein in press; Waite, Leibowitz, and

Witsberger in press) have reported virtually no relationship between parent preferences and these quality dimensions. Aspects of care associated with location, hours, and dependability predominate in these latter reports. Perhaps a two-stage process is involved, in which parents consider convenience and price when selecting a particular type of care, and then consider developmental aspects of care if they have more than one option that meets their initial criteria. It may also be the case that factors influencing selection and those influencing satisfaction with a selected arrangement differ. These issues warrant further empirical study, as do questions about whether and how parents establish and use various criteria when searching for child care. Can they recognize a well-qualified provider? Do they inquire about staff turnover? Do they allow the necessary time when searching to identify appropriate daily activities? Knowledge that is not utilized in the child care search is as ineffective as ignorance.

Regulations per se do not eliminate low-quality centers. Several states have exceedingly minimal regulations that fall far below any set of national quality guidelines that have been proposed (Phillips, Lande, and Goldberg 1990). Moreover, the monitoring of compliance with regulations is spotty at best, creating wide variation in quality even in states with acceptable regulations. Evidence for this wide variation in licensed centers emerged from the National Child Care Staffing Study (Whitebook, Howes, and Phillips 1990). For example, while a ratio of one adult per four infants is considered acceptable in the child care field, 16 percent of the infant classrooms in this study were observed to have one adult caring for more than five infants. A more global assessment of quality based on observations of classroom safety, equipment, and activities revealed that the average classroom in the sample was rated as falling at a "barely adequate" level of quality. For all ages of children, close to one-third or more of the classrooms received a scale score indicating "minimally adequate" care and at most, 12 percent of the classrooms met or exceeded a scale score indicating "good" care. Thus, regulations do not eliminate low-quality centers before start-up, as Walker suggests. It is the stringency, coverage, and enforcement of regulations that affect quality of care.

Taken together, these findings suggest that both hidden action and adverse selection may characterize the center care market. As Walker notes, hidden action occurs under conditions where consumers cannot perfectly monitor the providers. Questions about whether parents know how to or are able to apply their ideas about child care quality when searching for child care are directly pertinent to this aspect of imperfect information. Additionally, the neighborhood basis of child care centers, the niche-building approach of the lower-quality for-profit chains, and the inadequacy with which regulations assure a minimum level of quality in child care centers suggest that conditions are ripe for adverse selection, in which low-quality providers are selected into the child care market.

With respect to incomplete markets, I strongly endorse Walker's cautions about using waiting-list data as a proxy for demand. This is particularly the case in the absence of efforts to determine when these lists were last updated. I also support the importance of examining subsidies as a crucial component of understanding how fees are related to costs and services. However, I am less convinced than Walker that many child care centers are "highly subsidized by private groups or government funding." The National Child Care Staffing Study data revealed that government funding as a proportion of total center revenues dropped from 29 percent to 18 percent between 1977 and 1988. Other sources of funding, including corporate and charitable contributions, constituted a trivial 5 percent share of center revenues. This issue is prominent in debates about the advantages and disadvantages that the child care market offers nonprofit and for-profit centers. It is not well recognized that for-profit centers are eligible for government subsidies. Among our for-profit chains, for example, an average 11 percent of center revenues are derived from government subsidies. For independent, for-profit centers this figure was 7 percent. Secondly, the for-profit chains are likely to benefit from other financial advantages such as economies of scale and real estate investments (some invest in their child care buildings). Questions about the distribution of internal and external subsidies across various types of child care centers, and their effects on fees and services, are richly deserving of research attention.

QUESTIONS OF EQUITY

Finally, I want to urge economists to include issues of equity in their efforts to evaluate the functioning of the child care market. Walker suggests that families with higher incomes can "obtain" higher quality care. Certainly they can purchase higher quality care, as quality varies positively with price. But, contrary to common perceptions, the National Child Care Staffing Study revealed that quality care is not directly and positively associated with household income. In general, we found substantial evidence of social stratification in child care centers, but it was middle-income families that were the least likely to obtain higher quality care. Low-income families were more likely to obtain higher quality care than were middle-income families, but were less likely to obtain quality care than were high-income families. Not surprisingly, high-income families paid substantially more for care than did all other families. However, low-income families who paid for care paid somewhat higher fees than did middle-income families. These indicators of inequity in terms of quality and price should be of concern to both economic analysts and policymakers.

CONCLUSION

I have attempted to shed some additional light on the comments and assumptions made by Walker, to bring some additional realities about the child care market to bear on his framework, and to add to the agenda concerns about equity. It is important not to lose sight of the fact that Walker's paper constitutes an important contribution to our thinking about the child care market. His repeated calls to examine this market as heterogeneous, to question traditional economic assumptions about markets, and also to question simplistic criticisms that "the market" is not working should become integral to all child care research. As he notes, policymakers need to know in what ways, for which consumers, and in which sectors the child care market works and does not work. The notion of "perfect" anything—let alone market perfection—is quite foreign to the child care field. Perhaps serious analysis along the lines proposed by Walker can achieve better, if not perfect, child care.

REFERENCES

Blau, David. 1990. "The Child Care Labor Market." *Journal of Human Resources*, forthcoming, Winter 1992.

Coelen, C., F. Glantz, and D. Calore. 1978. *Day Care Centers in the U.S.: A National Profile, 1976–1977.* Cambridge, MA: Abt Associates.

Hayes, C. D., J. L. Palmer, and M. J. Zaslow, eds. 1990. *Who Cares for America's Children? Child Care Policy for the 1990's*. Washington, DC: National Academy Press.

Hofferth, Sandra L., and D. A. Wissoker. 1990. "Quality, Price and Income in Child Care Choice." Unpublished manuscript. Washington, DC: Urban Institute.

Phillips, D., ed. 1987. *Quality in Child Care: What Does Research Tell Us?* Washington, DC: National Association for the Education of Young Children.

Phillips, D., J. Lande, and M. Goldberg. 1990. "The State of Child Care Regulation." *Early Childhood Research Quarterly*. Vol. 5: 151–179.

Shinn, M., E. Galinsky, and L. Gulcur. 1989. "The Role of Child Care Centers in the Lives of Parents." Paper presented at the Biennial Conference on Community Research and Action, East Lansing, MI.

Shinn, M., D. Phillips, C. Howes, E. Galinsky, and M. Whitebook. 1990. "Correspondence Between Mothers' Perceptions and Observer Ratings of Quality in Child Care Centers." Unpublished manuscript. New York University.

Sonenstein, Freya L. 1991. "The Child Care Preferences of Parents with Young Children: How Little Is Known." In *Parental Leave and Child Care: Setting a Research and Policy Agenda*, edited by Janet Hyde and Marilyn Essex. Philadelphia: Temple University Press. 337–353.

Waite, L., A. Leibowitz, and C. Witsberger. 1991. "What Parents Pay For: Child Care Characteristics, Quality, and Costs." *Journal of Social Issues* 47, 2.

Walker, J. R. 1990. "New Evidence on the Supply of Child Care: A Statistical Portrait of Family Providers and an Analysis of Their Fees." Unpublished manuscript. Department of Economics and Institute for Research on Poverty, University of Wisconsin, Madison. *Journal of Human Resources*, forthcoming, Winter 1992.

Whitebook, M., C. Howes, and D. Phillips. 1990. "Who Cares? Child Care Teachers and the Quality of Care in America." Final report of the National Child Care Staffing Study. Berkeley, CA: The Child Care Employee Project.

4

The Importance of Child Care Costs to Women's Decision Making

Rachel Connelly

The national debate on child care policy has identified three areas of concern—accessibility, affordability, and quality. Discussions of accessibility focus on the family's ability to find appropriate child care. Many have argued that there is a shortage of child care options available to parents. Advocates of this position point to long waiting lists in child care centers and long parental searches to arrange care. A particular problem area appears to be the availability of infant care.

The problem with the quality of care is that child-development experts feel that much of the child care available in the United States is of poor quality. These experts point to the large percentage of children cared for in unlicensed home care and to the lack of training of many of these home care providers. They are also concerned with the low wages of child care providers and the high rate of staff turnover at child care centers. Parents seem less unhappy with the quality of care their children are receiving. In a recent survey, about 70 percent said they were satisfied with their child care arrangement (Kisker et al. 1989). Even if parents are satisfied with the quality of care, it is possible that the quality of care is too low when we take into account the effect of high quality child care on the future achievement of children. Some studies have shown large payoffs to early childhood education especially for children already at a disadvantage from poverty and/or family disruption.

Discussions of affordability center on the family's ability to pay for child care. A substantial part of a young family's budget is devoted to child care expenses. For families with at least one child under age 13 where the mother is employed and pays for child care, 8 percent of the family's monthly income is devoted to child care. Child care expenses make up 20 percent of the earnings of employed mothers with at least one child under 13, who pay for care. The percent of family income devoted to child care increases as incomes decline. Families with a yearly income less than $10,000 in 1985, who paid for care, paid 27 percent of their income for child care; those with incomes over $50,000 who paid for care devoted only 4 percent of their income to child care. As a result, concerns about the affordability of child care are often focused on families in the lower end of the income distribution.

While this trilogy of accessibility, affordability, and quality is appealing, I believe it masks the underlying economic factors that are common to all three areas. In other words, by separating the issue in this way, we fail to see that all three concerns are really part of the same issue—the effect of the cost of child care on family decision making. It is not hard to see that affordability is essentially concerned with the cost of child care and the impact of those costs on the family's disposable income. Child care costs are also at the heart of the accessibility issue. The problem parents have in finding child care is really the problem of finding child care at a price the family is willing to pay. Presumably, one would have no difficulty finding care for an infant if one offered an amount comparable to the annual salary of an elementary school teacher. On the other hand, very few families can find a full-time caregiver for their infant at no cost. Parents differ in the amount they are willing or able to pay for infant care, and those willing to pay only a small amount will have difficulty finding care. Thus, the problem of accessibility is not the result of an inherent shortage of child care at any price, but, rather, that many families find child care inaccessible because they are unwilling or unable to pay the market price for the quality of child care they want.

The problem of quality is also really a problem of costs. Although experts may differ on what constitutes high quality care, there is a general consensus that lower child-to-staff ratios and higher levels of staff training are positively related to higher quality care. Both these criteria lead to higher labor costs for high quality care. Thus, high quality care costs more to provide than low quality care and parents face a continuum of price/quality combinations of child care from which to choose. If all levels of quality cost the same, all families would choose high quality care for their children. However, given the price/quality continuum, some families, because of budget pressures, will choose lower priced/lower quality care over higher priced/higher quality care.

As quality, accessibility, and affordability are all fundamentally related to the cost of child care, understanding the determinants of the cost of child care and the effect of child care costs on the family's choices is essential to our ability to formulate good child care policy. This chapter seeks to address the issue of costs by focusing on the following questions: (1) How much do families pay for child care? (2) What factors determine the amount of money devoted to child care? (3) What is the effect of the amount paid on the mother's decision whether to participate in the labor market? In attempting to answer these questions, the chapter concentrates primarily on my work with the Survey of Income and Program Participation (SIPP). However, I have tried, whenever possible, to include evidence from other researchers who have addressed these same issues. The advantage of SIPP for this type of analysis is that the data are quite recent, December 1984 through March 1985, and that SIPP is a nationally representative survey of about 16,000 households. The major disadvantage is that the child care expenditure data are collected per family instead of per child. This makes it difficult to discuss the cost of child care per child. However, our focus here is on the family, not the child, and the data are appropriate for this purpose.

WHO IS PAYING WHAT FOR CHILD CARE?

To investigate the amount families are paying for child care, we need to define the sample of families for whom child care expenditures are a relevant consideration. To this end I have chosen the set of families who have at least one child under age 13, in which the mother is between 21 and 55 and is employed in the most recent month of the survey period.[1] Families in this

---

[1] We can quibble about the age at which children no longer need child care. I have chosen 12 as a cutoff because many 13-year-olds are already babysitting for younger children. Empirically, we find that very few parents whose youngest child is 10 to 12 pay for child care. I have limited the sample to mothers over 21 in an attempt to avoid most of the cases in which the mother is still in school. This is necessary because the child care data in SIPP are restricted to employed mothers, yet we know that child care is often used so that young mothers can continue their education.

sample differ substantially in the amount they pay for child care. We hypothesize that differences come from the number and ages of the children, the number of hours the mother works, the quality of care purchased, and the availability of no-cost[2] child care arrangements. Families with older children may allow children to stay by themselves after school. Families with younger children may have relatives in the household or nearby who are willing to care for the children without a cash payment. Some families may be able to arrange work schedules so that the husband or other family members can care for the children while the mother is away from the house.[3] Differences in expenditures may also come from the type of care used, the local price level, and the location of residence. For example, families in metropolitan areas who pay for care pay more on average than families living in nonmetropolitan areas.

For the entire sample, the average weekly expenditure on child care is $15 a week. Readers who are currently paying for child care are now shaking their heads, saying this figure is too low. This figure appears low because over 60 percent of the sample does not pay for care. Table 1 shows the entire distribution of expenditures. If we look at just those families paying for care, the average weekly expenditure is $40, an amount comparable to the findings of Moore and Hofferth (1979), Fosburg et al. (1981), Coelen et al. (1979), Hofferth (1988), and Kisker et al. (1989), once we adjust for changes in the value of a dollar over time.[4] For example, in their study of three low-income urban areas, Kisker et al. found that the median total cost of child care for mothers paying for care was $50 a week in 1988. These costs also correspond to the costs reported by child care centers and family day care homes in Kisker et al. Child care centers reported fees of $35 to $50 per week for toddlers and older preschoolers. They charge more for infants but less for children from low-income families.

As 60 percent of families do not pay cash for care, we are interested in the percent who report a formal noncash arrangement. The survey question reads, "Did you pay for any child care through a noncash arrangement, such as providing room and board or exchanging child care services?" For the entire sample,

---

[2] By this we mean no money cost, since we expect that all child care arrangements involve nonmonetary costs, some explicitly stated, others not.

[3] See Presser (1986).

[4] The results of Moore and Hofferth (1979), Fosburg et al. (1981), Coelen et al. (1979), and Hofferth (1988) were presented in Hofferth (1988).

TABLE 1

*Distribution of Weekly Expenditures for all Employed Women
Aged 21–55 with at Least One Child under 13*

Weekly Expenditure for Child Care	All Families	Those Paying for Care
0	63.6%	—
1–9	1.3	3.5
10–19	4.2	11.6
20–29	7.2	19.7
30–39	6.9	18.9
40–49	5.6	15.4
50–59	4.7	12.9
60–69	2.2	6.0
70–79	1.6	4.4
80–89	.7	2.0
90+	2.0	5.6
Mean Expenditure	15	40
Median Expenditure	0	35

SOURCE: SIPP 1984 Panel, 5th Wave.

only 3 percent answered yes to this question. Of those, 59 percent report having a noncash arrangement only; 41 percent report paying in cash and in kind.

The percent of families paying for care differs substantially by family characteristics. Table 2 shows some of these differences. Families with at least one child under age 6 are substantially more likely to pay for care. The average is 59 percent compared to the 13 percent of families with the youngest child aged 6 to 12. Many of the families with older children use school as the primary child care arrangement, followed, if need be, by self-care or care by an older sibling. Notice that families with a teenager are substantially less likely to pay for care.

The percent of families with children under 13, paying for care, increases as the number of children needing care goes from one to two but then declines as the number of children increases beyond two. The percent of families using noncash arrangements increases substantially as the number of children increases. As the cost of formal child care increases with the number of children one has, parents with more children looking for less costly forms of child care appear to be more likely to use noncash arrangements. Alternatively, it may be that noncash arrangements, such as a live-in child care provider, make more economic sense when there are a large number of children. The fact that 8 per-

TABLE 2
Percent of Families with Employed Mothers Aged 21–55 Paying for Child Care

	Families with at Least One Child <13			Families with at Least One Child <6		
	% Paying Cash Only	% Paying Cash and Non-Cash	% Paying Non-Cash Only	% Paying Cash Only	% Paying Cash and Non-Cash	% Paying Non-Cash Only
Total	35.1	1.2	1.7	56.5	2.1	2.2
Number of Children						
1	31.9	0.5	1.7	59.5	0.7	2.1
2	40.5	1.9	1.2	57.9	3.2	1.6
3	34.0	1.9	2.6	46.4	2.7	3.6
4+	30.8	2.6	5.1	34.3	2.9	5.7
Another Adult Woman in the Family	20.0	3.6	3.6	34.8	7.6	4.3
No Other Adult Woman in the Family	36.8	0.9	1.5	58.6	1.5	1.9
Adult Man in Family (other than husband)	18.7	1.3	2.0	32.3	3.2	1.6
No Other Adult Man in the Family	36.5	1.2	1.7	58.1	2.0	2.2

Teenage Children					
13–18 in the Family	12.7	0.5	1.8	42.0	2.5	5.9
No Child 13–18	44.8	1.5	1.6	58.4	2.0	1.7
Married	34.9	1.2	1.6	55.5	2.2	2.2
Unmarried	36.1	1.1	2.0	60.7	1.6	2.1
Family Income						
0–$9,999	31.2	0.7	2.8	50.8	1.5	3.1
$10,000–19,999	34.6	0.5	1.7	51.1	0.5	2.7
20,000–29,999	31.4	1.9	1.2	52.4	3.5	1.7
30,000–39,999	35.0	1.8	1.8	56.4	3.0	1.3
40,000–49,999	41.5	0.4	0.8	68.5	0.8	1.6
50,000+	38.8	1.0	2.2	63.3	2.0	3.4
Residence in:						
SMSA	34.6	0.9	1.6	54.5	1.6	1.6
Not in SMSA	35.8	1.5	1.8	58.5	2.6	2.8
Northeast	30.5	0.4	2.0	50.0	0.9	3.3
Central	36.0	1.3	1.5	54.6	1.9	2.3
South	36.7	0.9	1.2	64.5	1.4	1.4
West	36.9	2.6	2.6	52.0	4.5	2.0

SOURCE: SIPP 1984 Panel, 5th Wave.

cent of those parents with four or more children who are paying for care also have a noncash arrangement lends support to this latter view.[5]

The increase in the percent paying for care from one child to two is probably related to the age distribution of the children—having two children under age 13, it is more likely that one of them needs formal care outside school. When the youngest child is less than 6 we do not observe the change in the percent paying for care between one and two children. However, we continue to find the large drop in the percent paying for care as the number of children increases above two. This decline in the percent paying for care is evidence of the selection process underlying all these numbers. Recall that our sample is a sample of employed mothers. Women without the option of no-cost child care face substantially higher child care costs with more children. Many of these women, when faced with these high child care costs, choose not to participate in the labor market. Thus, in looking at a sample of women who are in the labor market, we expect those women with no-cost child care options to be overrepresented in groups for whom formal child care costs are especially high. In a multivariate analysis of the determinants of child care expenditures we can control for this selection process by jointly estimating the decision to be employed with whether one pays for care. We will discuss this type of analysis later.

Returning to Table 2, we have already noted the diminished probability of paying for child care if there is a teenager present in the family. The presence of an adult woman other than the mother, or an adult male other than the husband, also lowers the probability of paying for child care; and married women are slightly less likely to pay for care, presumably because of the presence of the husband as a potential caregiver. On the other hand, family income is higher for married women, and higher family income is related to a slightly increased probability of paying for care, especially for families with a child under age 6.

Table 3 reports the average amount paid for child care for all those families paying for care and the percent of family income and the mother's own earnings that are spent on child care. The average weekly expenditure on child care increases with the number of children in the family, as does the percent of family income devoted to child care. Families with other potential care-

---

[5] The number of families with four or more children in our sample is quite small, making conclusions about families with a large number of young children tentative.

givers present—adult women, adult men, or teenagers—pay less for care. Married women pay more per week for child care than unmarried women but devote a smaller percent of family income to child care. This is because family income levels are substantially higher for married than for unmarried women.[6]

The amount paid for child care increases with total family income, perhaps indicating that high-income families choose higher quality care. An alternative explanation is that families have higher incomes because the mother works more hours in the labor market. This would also lead to higher child care expenditures. Whatever the motivation, high-income families allocate a smaller percent of their family income to child care expenses than do low-income families. Families who pay for care in the lowest income category with incomes of less than $10,000 devoted more than 25 percent of family income to child care. This amount is over 30 percent of the mother's labor earnings. Except for this very low income group, a family's child care expenses as a percent of the mother's earnings average about 18 percent. There appears to be little pattern in the relationship between family income and the percent of mother's earnings going to child care.

Because the SIPP survey question on child care expenditures asked for total family expenditures on child care, it is not possible, using the whole sample, to explore how expenditures differ by type of child care used. However, we can gain some insight into expenditure by type of child care if we limit ourselves to families with only one child. SIPP collects information on two types of child care arrangements per child, so we must further limit ourselves to families with only one child and who use only one kind of paid child care.[7] This restricted sample allows us to look at differences in child care expenditures by the age of the child and differences by the type of child care used.

Table 4 summarizes that data for families with only one child in at most one type of paid care. As we predicted, the percent of

---

[6] See Connelly (1989b) for a more detailed comparison of weekly child care expenditures of married and unmarried women.

[7] This is less restrictive than the sample used by the U.S. Bureau of the Census (1987). In that study, which uses the same SIPP data, they restricted the analysis to those with only one child and only one type of child care listed. I have included those with two types of care if one or both of them were in a category usually thought to be unpaid, such as self-care or care by the husband or older children. My results do differ from Bureau of the Census (1987) for older children, who are very likely to list two types of care, one of which is elementary school. By excluding these children, a very specialized group of older children remained in the census sample.

TABLE 3

Average Weekly Expenditure on Child Care for Those Families Paying for Care

	Families with Children Under 13			Families with Children Under 6		
	Average	% of Family Income	% of Mother's Earnings	Average	% of Family Income	% of Mother's Earnings
Total Number of Children						
1	35.36	7	15	39.61	8	17
2	43.64	9	21	45.81	9	22
3	46.55	10	26	47.15	10	26
4+	51.00	7	69	51.00	7	69
Other Adult Woman Present	36.07	6	19	37.41	9	22
No Other Adult Woman Present	40.25	8	20	43.74	6	20
Other Adult Male Present	29.53	7	15	31.09	9	22
No Other Adult Male Present	40.43	8	20	43.79	4	17

Teenager Present	32.05	6	16	36.26	7	19
No Teenager Present	40.95	9	20	44.01	9	22
Married	41.27	7	20	44.51	7	22
Not Married	35.65	13	17	38.55	14	19
Family Income						
0–$9,999	28.47	27	31	30.71	30	34
$10,000–19,999	34.70	12	21	35.16	12	23
20,000–29,999	35.36	7	19	38.59	8	21
30,000–39,999	42.50	6	21	45.97	7	23
40,000–49,999	42.44	5	14	45.38	5	15
50,000+	50.89	4	18	57.98	4	20
SMSA	44.59	8	21	49.26	9	24
Not in SMSA	35.63	8	18	37.83	8	20
Regions						
Northeast	44.34	9	20	50.46	10	23
Central	37.53	8	22	42.18	8	26
South	39.13	8	18	40.32	8	19
West	40.67	9	18	44.10	8	19
Total	39.98	8	20	43.32	9	22

SOURCE: SIPP 1984 Panel, 5th Wave.

TABLE 4

Families with One Child Under 13 in at most One Type of Paid Care

	% Paying Cash Only	% Paying Cash and Non-Cash	% Paying Non-Cash Only	Average Weekly Expenses	Those Who Pay	
					Average Hourly Expenses Per Hour Care Used	Average Hourly Expenses Per Hour Worked
Total	32.5	0.6	1.8	34.97	1.41	0.96
Age of Child						
0–2	57.2	0.5	2.9	41.25	1.23	1.14
3–5	65.8	1.0	1.5	37.41	1.13	1.02
6–9	24.4	1.1	3.1	24.39	2.05	0.68
10–12	6.7	0	0.5	20.40	2.03	0.50
Type of Care Used						
Relative in child's home	21.3	1.3	5.3	18.82	1.95	0.58
Relative in other's home	52.0	0	2.5	29.71	0.99	0.84
Nonrelative in child's home	71.4	9.5	4.8	39.18	1.46	1.13
Nonrelative in other's home	85.0	1.4	4.1	34.83	1.52	0.93
Group care	79.0	0.6	2.8	38.19	1.36	1.04

SOURCE: SIPP 1984 Panel, 5th Wave.

families paying for care depends greatly on the age of the child. Of those families whose child is 3 to 5 years old, over 65 percent pay for care, while only 7 percent of families whose child is 10 to 12 years of age pay for care. Noncash arrangements are slightly more common for infants and for 6- to 9-year-olds than other age groups. For families who pay for care, average weekly expenditures decline as the child ages. There is a large gap in average weekly expenditures between preschoolers and school-aged children as the number of hours spent in paid care is greater for preschool children.

Because children in this sample have only one kind of paid care we can calculate average hourly expenditure per hour in paid care. Cost per hour of care is higher for older children. This corresponds to a finding by Kisker et al. that family day care providers "tend to charge substantially higher hourly rates for part-time than full-time care" [Kisker et al., p. 16, Executive Summary]. In a multivariate analysis using the SIPP data, I found that the cost per hour of care declined as the number of hours of care increased, controlling for the age of the child and the type of care used.

Table 4 also shows differences in expenditure patterns across types of child care used. Only 28 percent of the sample paid cash or in-kind payments to relatives who cared for their child at home. Fifty-five percent made a cash or in-kind payment to a relative who cared for the child at the relative's home. On the other side of the spectrum, the vast majority of transactions with nonrelatives and group care involve some kind of a payment. One interesting finding is the large percent of arrangements involving a nonrelative in the child's home that include both cash and in-kind payments.

Looking at the amount paid per type of care, there appears to be little difference in money cost among nonrelative care in the home, nonrelative care in the caregiver's home, and group care. However, 12 percent of the families paying for nonrelative care in their own home also make a noncash payment so the total cost of this arrangement will be more than the other types of care. The lowest cost option from the perspective of cost per hour of care is relative care in the relative's home at approximately $1.00 per hour.

To summarize our findings in this section we return to the section heading "Who is paying what for child care?" Tables 1 through 4 give us hundreds of numbers in an attempt to answer this question. The major findings are:

1. From Table 1 we learned that looking at the average expenditures levels for all families led to a very low estimate of weekly child care expenditure because of the large number of families who do not pay for care. Therefore, we divided our analysis into two parts: in Table 2, we examined differences in who pays for care, and in Table 3, we looked at the amount paid for care by those who pay for care.

2. Paying for care is related to having fewer children and younger children. Families with other potential caregivers are less likely to pay for care, whereas those with higher incomes are more likely to pay for care.

3. The amount paid for care increases with the number of children and with income. Expenditures as a percent of family income increase slightly as the number of children increases and declines as family income increases. The percent of the mother's earnings devoted to child care is quite substantial, 20 percent on average, and does not differ much from category to category.

4. A more limited sample of families with only one child in, at most, one type of paid care was used to look at the effect of age of the child and type of child care on expenditures. Since there is only one kind of paid care, we were able to calculate the cost per hour in paid care. Results show that the probability of paying for care declines dramatically for school-aged children. Parents of 3- to 5-year-olds are the most likely to pay for care. Average weekly expenditures are less for school-aged children because of the hours spent in school, but the cost per hour of care is higher.

5. Relative care is less likely to be paid for than nonrelative care or group care. For those who pay for care, the costs per hour are similar for all kinds of care, with relative care in the relative's home being the least costly and relative care in the child's home being the most costly. However, over 70 percent of relative care in the child's home is not paid for, either in cash or in kind.

RESULTS OF A MULTIVARIATE ANALYSIS OF CHILD CARE EXPENDITURES

The information presented in the section above gives us a thorough picture of the distribution of child care expenditures in the winter of 1985. However, tables of this type cannot be used to determine causal links between family characteristics and child care expenditures. For example, family income may increase expenditures as the result of an increase in the quality of care purchased or because of the underlying relationship between family income and the number of hours a woman works in the labor market. In addition, we mentioned the problem of self-selection into the sample. Those women who have no-cost child care options are more likely to be working, and, thus, are more likely to appear in the sample. In order to fully understand the determinants of child care expenditures, we must consider the effect of a given characteristic on expenditures, holding all other characteristics constant. This section summarizes the results of this type of statistical analysis of weekly child care expenditures. The results presented here were originally reported in Connelly (1989b). Relevant tables from that paper are included in the Appendix to this chapter as Tables A-1 and A-2. The sample is the same as that used in the previous section.

To deal with the problem of self-selection, the probability of paying for care was estimated jointly with the probability of being employed. The correlation between these two events is approximately − .5. This means that, after all else is accounted for, those women who are less likely to pay for child care are more likely to be employed. Thus, as we suspected, those with no-cost child care options are more likely to appear in the sample, especially those women for whom formal child care costs would be quite large.

Among the factors that were found to affect the probability of paying for care are the number of children aged 0 to 2 and aged 3 to 5. An additional child in either age group increases the probability of paying for care. For married women, increasing the number of children aged 6 to 12 decreases the probability of paying for care. For unmarried women, an additional 6- to 12-year-old has no effect on the probability of paying for child care.

The presence of a teenager was found to decrease the probability of paying for care for both unmarried and married women. For unmarried women, the presence of a not-employed adult woman also decreases the probability of paying. For married women, the presence of an adult man other than the husband decreases the probability of paying, as does the presence of an unemployed adult male, including the husband. For married women, a higher level of nonlabor income[8] increases the proba-

---

[8] This is defined as family income minus the mother's labor earnings. It is largely the husband's earnings.

bility of paying. For unmarried women the amount of nonlabor income is quite small, and the amount available has no discernible effect on the probability of paying.

Factors found not to be related to the probability of paying, once we control for all other variables, include the level of education of the mother, the race of the mother, the region of residence, residence in a metropolitan area, and the cost of living in the state of residence. The last three factors are thought to affect the amount of expenditure but not the probability of expenditure.

After correcting for the probability of paying for care and the probability of being employed, we used women who were both employed and paying for care to estimate the effect of family characteristics on the amount paid for child care. The sample was divided into married and unmarried women, since women in these two groups were thought to differ substantially because of large differences in family income and because of the presence of, or lack of, a husband as a potential caregiver. For both married and unmarried women, we found evidence of differences in weekly child care expenditures based on the number of preschool children in the family and on location of residence. Increasing the number of preschool children increases weekly child care expenses. The effect of additional children under age 6 is larger for unmarried women than for married women. For unmarried women, an additional child, newborn to 2 years of age, adds $7.44 per week to child care expenses. For married women, the amount added is $3.60. Living in a metropolitan area increases one's expenditure by about $2.70 a week. Living in a state with a higher cost of living also increases expenditures, although the effect is small. For married women, residence in the central or northeastern regions of the United States significantly decreases weekly expenditures compared to those living in the West, while those living in the South pay more than those in the West. The pattern is the same for unmarried women, but the estimates were less precise.

This is a good time to remind the reader of the "everything else held constant" nature of these results. Living in the South often means a lower cost of living. As we stated above, this tends to decrease child care expenditures. However, holding the cost of living constant, living in the South tends to increase child care expenses. The net effect of these two findings will depend on the actual state of residence and its cost of living.

Important differences between the determinants of unmarried

and married women's child care expenditure occur in the effect of education and hours worked on expenditure. Increased levels of education have a significant positive impact on expenditures for married women but an insignificant effect for unmarried women. Conversely, hours worked have a small but positive impact on the expenditures for unmarried women and an insignificant effect on married women's expenditures. These results can be interpreted as differences between married and unmarried women in the importance placed on the quality of care and on the price per unit of quality. As the level of education of the mother is not expected to change the price of child care, this variable probably affects the quality of care chosen. On the other hand, hours worked, along with the number of children in the family, are expected to directly affect the price of child care per unit of quality. Together the results on education, hours worked, and the number of young children suggest a stronger reliance by unmarried mothers on the type of care that is priced by the hour and by the child and suggest that unmarried mothers may be sacrificing on the quality of care purchased because they face a higher price per hour for child care.

The results of this multivariate analysis have refined but not essentially altered our conclusions from those earlier. Families differ a great deal in the costs they face for child care. Families with more young children are more likely to pay for child care and, if they pay, they pay more per week than families with older children. The presence of other potential caregivers lowers the probability of paying for care and thus lowers the expected cost of care. The education of the mother does not affect the probability of paying, but it does increase the amount paid by married women. Locational differences also have a substantial effect on the level of weekly child care expenses.

At this point we return to the issues raised early in the chapter to ask the question, "Why should we care about differences in the costs of child care?" The answer is, we care because the cost of child care affects the level of disposable income available to the family and a large number of choices made by the family. These choices are several, such as how many children to have, whether the mother participates in the formal labor market, whether a family receives Aid to Families with Dependent Children (AFDC), the quality of child care purchased, and the level of income available to meet other needs of the family. In other words, the cost of child care for a particular family affects the accessibility, affordability, and quality of care purchased. In the next section we sketch out the mechanism by which child care costs affect the family's decision making.

THE EFFECT OF CHILD CARE COSTS ON THE FAMILY—THEORETICAL FRAMEWORK

Child care costs become part of the family's decision making in two ways. First, child care costs can be thought of as a part of the cost of rearing a child and so affect decisions in which the cost of children is a relevant factor. In addition, child care costs lower the mother's effective wage in the labor market, and thus affect decisions for which the mother's wage is a relevant factor.

In terms of the cost of children, one could argue that the higher the cost of child care, the higher the cost of an additional child. This leads us to predict that higher child care costs will tend to lower fertility. However, we must recall that since paid child care is used as a substitute for family care (usually for the mother's own time), formal child care lowers the total cost of a child especially for mothers with a high earnings capacity. Thus, although increasing the cost of child care increases the cost per child, it will not increase the cost beyond the cost per child that would be relevant if no extrafamily child care were used. As a result, we expect the impact of child care costs on the cost of a child to be quite limited.

Once the fertility decision has been made, the major impact of child care costs is on the effective wage of the mother. To see why, we separate the family's decision about the use of extrafamily child care into two parts. First, the family decides who will care for the children if no extrafamily child care is used. We call this family member the "designated caregiver." Then the family decides if the "designated caregiver" will care for the children or if extrafamily child care will be used. If we assume that family members are indifferent about who among them will care for the children in the absence of extrafamily child care, we expect that each family will choose the member with the lowest market earnings potential as the "designated caregiver." In most families, especially in nuclear families, the member with the lowest market earnings potential is the mother. If, in addition, families are not indifferent about who cares for the children and either believe that children are better off being cared for by their mother than by their father, or if the mother enjoys child care responsibilities more than the father, then it is even more likely that the "designated caregiver" will be the mother. Note, though, that these latter criteria are not necessary for the result. Fuchs (1989) has argued that women are affected more by child care costs because they have a higher demand for child care, not because they care more about child welfare than men do. But here we see that if they have the same demand for child care but lower wages than men, they will still be the "designated caregiver," and thus, the decision to use extrafamily child care will be affected by their wages alone.

For the purposes of our discussion we will assume that, in every case, the mother is the family's "designated caregiver." The second stage of the family's child care decision is the decision of whether the mother, as "designated caregiver," will work in the market and use extrafamily child care. The mother bases her decision on the costs and benefits of working in the labor market, and these will depend on her wage minus the cost per hour worked of child care. We call her wage, minus the cost per hour worked of child care, her effective wage. Increasing the cost of extrafamily child care decreases her effective wage. A decrease in her effective wage unambiguously decreases the probability of participating in the labor market. If she is still participating in the labor market, a decline in her effective wage has two offsetting effects on the number of hours she will work. A decrease in the wage lowers the amount of family income, which alone has the effect of increasing the number of hours she will work in the market. But the decrease in the wage also lowers the value of an extra hour spent in the labor market relative to the value of an extra hour spent at home, which leads her to substitute away from labor market time toward home time. For women with children, the substitution effect is expected to dominate the income effect, leading to the prediction that the number of hours worked in the labor market should decrease as the cost of child care increases.

Recall that the cost of child care differs substantially among families, based on the location of residence and the number of young children in the family. Thus, we expect that mothers with more and/or younger children will be less likely to work in the labor market simply because they face higher child care costs. If they continue to work in the labor market, they will work fewer hours. We expect that the effect of child care costs will be larger on participation than on hours worked because women may not be able to adjust their hours in the labor market to exactly equal their preferred number of hours.

The cost of child care can be thought of, in large part, as a cost of employment. However, part of the cost of child care depends on the quality of care chosen. To the extent that high quality child care leads to "higher quality" children, part of the expenditure on child care must be considered consumption. Families will choose the level of quality based on the costs and benefits of quality care compared with the costs and benefits of other consumption items. The larger the quality component of child care, the less negative we expect the effect of child care costs on a mother's labor market decisions to be. Evidence reported in an earlier section led us to hypothesize that weekly child care expenditures in two-parent families are more sensitive to quality considerations, and thus we expect that the labor supplied by married women with young children will be less sensitive to the child care expenditures than the labor supply of unmarried mothers.

As we have predicted that increased child care cost decreases the probability of participating in the labor market, increased child care cost should also increase the probability that unmarried mothers will receive AFDC. Understanding the effect of family characteristics on child care costs allows us to predict that women with younger children will be more likely to receive AFDC because they face higher child care costs. Women with higher potential wages should be less likely to receive AFDC, controlling for the child care costs, since their effective wage is higher. Once we have controlled for child care costs, it would be interesting to see if any effect of the number of children on AFDC recipiency remains.

Several recent studies have been completed to test the predictions offered in this section: Heckman (1974), Blau and Robins (1988, 1989a, 1989b), Connelly (1989a, 1989b, 1990), and Ribar (1990). In the next section we review the findings from these papers.

THE EFFECT OF CHILD CARE COSTS
ON THE FAMILY—EMPIRICAL FINDINGS

Most of the studies listed above are concerned with estimating the labor supply effects of child care costs. These are the results on which I will concentrate. Two recent papers (1989a, 1989b) by Blau and Robins look at the effect of child care costs on fertility. Both studies find a negative effect of child care costs of fertility. The two papers use different data sets, so the confirmation from both papers is encouraging. It is difficult to get any sense of the magnitude of this effect, although it does not appear to be very large.

A great many studies show a negative effect of the presence of young children on the labor supply of the mother. The question we would like to answer is, how much of the negative effect of young children on the mother's labor supply is due to the increased cost of child care and how much is due to the increased value of the mother's time at home. This distinction is especially important in trying to assess the impact of child care policy on family choices. To analyze the effect of a child care program that subsidizes the cost of child care, child care costs must be explicitly included in the analysis.

All the papers we will discuss find that child care costs have a negative effect on the probability that the mother participates in the labor market. There is also some evidence that increased child care costs decrease the number of hours worked in the market. The studies differ substantially from one another in the sample of women included and in the way the cost of child care is calculated. Heckman, Blau and Robins, Connelly (1989a) and Ribar look only at two-parent families. Connelly (1989b) compares the labor supply effects of married and unmarried women. Connelly (1990) focuses exclusively on unmarried women and looks at the effect of child care costs on AFDC recipiency. The differences in the way the cost of child care is defined are the result of differences in type of data available to the researcher and the inherent complexity of the issue of child care costs. The complexity comes from the fact that if any data on child care costs is available, it is usually family child care expenditures. Expenditures depend on the level of quality chosen, which is itself a choice the family makes. In addition, the level of child care expenditure is available only for those families currently using child care. Yet all families face a cost of child care that they consider as part of their decision on whether the "designated caregiver" will participate in the labor market. How to assign a cost to these families is one of the major issues facing the researcher.

Heckman was the first economist to look explicitly at the issue of child care costs and their effect on married women's labor supply, and he did so without any information on the cost of child care! Heckman limited his analysis to married women from 30 to 44 with at least one child under 10. His data came from the National Longitudinal Survey, 1966. Although he had no data on family expenditure on child care, he did have information about whether families used formal or informal care, and, if they were not using care, whether they would use formal or informal care. Heckman set the cost of all formal care to one and assumed that the cost of informal care to each family is some number less than one. The amount by which the cost of informal care is less than one depends on the availability of alternative caregivers, which is estimated using variables such as the presence of children from 14 to 18, the presence of a relative in the household, the number of hours the husband worked, whether the woman had lived in the Standard Metropolitan Statistical Area (SMSA) all her life, and the length of residence in the SMSA. Thus, Heckman's estimated cost of child care allowed for differences in the availability of no-cost or low-cost care but did not include differences due to the number and age of the children and the location of residence. Heckman found a significant negative effect of his estimated cost of child care on labor supply. Controlling for the cost of child care, he found that additional young children continue to have a negative effect on labor supply. This effect diminishes substantially with the age of the child.

Blau and Robins (1988, 1989a) used data from the Employment Opportunity Pilot Projects, 1980, to estimate the effect of child care costs on the mother's labor supply. Their sample is defined as married women under age 45 with at least one child under 14. Their data does have information on the level of cash child care expenditure per family, but because they want to estimate the price per constant-quality hour of market child care per child, they average child care expenditures across families within a given geographical location. This is consistent with the notion that all families in the same geographical area face the same price per child for market child care. They also distinguish between those families using formal care, by which they mean paid care, and informal care. Because they averaged weekly expenditures within a geographical location, their cost of child care allows for differences in costs due to location but not for differences in a family's costs due to the number or age of the children.

In Blau and Robins (1988) they find that higher child care costs have a significant negative effect on the mother's employment and increase the probability of using informal care. Controlling for the average cost of child care in one's location of residence, the number of young children in the family still decreases the probability that the mother will work in the labor market. Based on the results of their estimation, Blau and Robins generated a set of predictions designed to show the size of the child care cost effect. They find that the probability that the average mother works is quite sensitive to the price of child care. If the price of child care were zero, in other words, if child care were fully subsidized, they find that 87 percent of the mothers would work. If child care cost $40 per week, the model predicts that only 19 percent would work.

In their 1989a paper Blau and Robins take advantage of the longitudinal nature of their data and look at the effect of child care costs on the probability of entering and leaving the labor market. They find that higher child care costs lead to an increased rate of leaving employment and a decreased rate of entering employment. A dollar increase in the average weekly child care costs is found to increase the rate of leaving employment by 2 percent. That same dollar increase is found to decrease by 3 percent the rate of not-employed women becoming employed. Like the results of Blau and Robins (1988), these results indicate fairly substantial labor supply effects.

Connelly (1989a) and Ribar used the SIPP data discussed earlier in the chapter. Connelly's sample is confined to women 21 to 55 years of age with at least one child under 13. Ribar uses a similar sample, which includes married couples with children under 15. A married women sample from SIPP is very similar to those of Heckman and Blau and Robins.[9] While the samples are similar, both Connelly and Ribar have chosen a very different method from either Heckman or Blau and Robins for assigning child care costs to all families. Connelly's approach is to estimate the determinants of child care costs from family characteristics. The results of that estimation process have already been discussed. After determining the impact of family characteristics on weekly expenditures, Connelly then estimates a level of family expenditure for each family, using what we know about the family. Using this method, an estimated cost of child care is attached to each woman in the sample, and we can then look at the impact of that expected child care cost on her labor market decisions. The estimated child care cost calculated in this way takes into account the potential for no-cost or low-cost informal

[9]Heckman's sample is substantially older, and the children are slightly younger, leading to bias toward families who have their children at older ages. The mean age of women in Blau and Robins's sample is 30.1; in Connelly's it is 33.0 for married women; in Ribar's it is 33.3.

care as Heckman's did by including the presence of other potential caregivers in the family. It also includes differences in the
cost due to location as Blau and Robins did by including locational variables such as residence in a metropolitan area, region
differences, and cost of living in the state of residence. In addition, these estimated child care costs include the effect of the
age and number of children in the household and include differences in the level of quality of child care that will be chosen by
the household.[10] Connelly (1989a) estimates the price of child
care per hour worked in order to control for the effect of hours
worked on the cost of child care.

Like Heckman and Blau and Robins, the results of the analysis
of married women (Connelly 1989a) show a significant negative
effect, on labor force participation, of increased child care cost
per hour worked. However, the magnitude of the effect is shown
to be smaller than Blau and Robins found. In Blau and Robins's
(1988) simulation to determine the size of the child care effect,
they used the characteristics of the average women in the sample
as the basis of the simulation. Using the same methodology,
Connelly too gets large changes in the percent in the labor force.
But a better measure of the effect of changing the price of child
care is to look at the effect of the change on each woman in
the sample.[11] Using the estimated cost of child care, the model
predicts that 58.8 percent of the women in the sample will be
employed. If universal no-cost child care were available, the
model predicts that 68.7 percent of the women would be employed. On reflection, the results are not too surprising when we
consider the large changes in women's labor force participation
rate over the last twenty-five years and the stability of child care
costs during that same period (Hofferth 1988). The increase in
women's labor force participation has certainly not been fueled
by sharp declines in child care costs.

One of the advantages of Connelly's method of estimating
the child care costs per family is that the independent effect of
additional children on women's labor force participation can
now be assessed. Results from Connelly (1989a) show that for

---

[10] The level of quality of child care is included only to the extent that it can be
proxied by the educational level of the mother and the level of nonlabor income in
the family.

[11] The technical difference between the two methods is that Blau and Robins
calculate the change in the probability that the average woman participates in the
market, whereas I compare the change in the mean probability of participating in
the market. In a linear model these two measures are the same, but they are not the
same in a nonlinear model such as the probit analysis used here.

married women, once we control for the price of child care, the number of young children in the family has no significant effect on the probability of participation.

Ribar uses a method similar to Connelly's to estimate a cost of child care for each family based on characteristics of the family and their state of residence. His measure differs from Connelly's in that it is an estimate of the hourly cost of *paid* child care per child (as opposed to Connelly's, which is the total cost of child care per hour that the mother is employed). Ribar finds a large negative effect of the cost of formal care on the labor supply of married women. These results differ from Connelly's in that they indicate a large response in married women's hours worked to a change in the price per hour of paid child care.

While married women constitute the majority of mothers of young children, they are not the group usually targeted in direct government subsidies of child care.[12] We saw earlier that a woman in the lowest income group was devoting over 25 percent of family income and over 30 percent of her own labor earnings to child care. Most of these women are single parents. The differences in expenditure by income suggest that the problem of high child care costs that leads to problems of affordability, accessibility, and quality may be more severe for single mothers. Connelly (1990) estimated the effect of child care cost on the labor force participation of unmarried mothers. Increased child care costs were shown to have a negative effect on the probability of labor force participation and a positive effect on the probability of receiving AFDC. Simulations show that subsidizing the cost of child care for single mothers would result in a substantial decrease in the number of women receiving AFDC payments. Moving to fully subsidized child care for unmarried mothers would reduce AFDC recipiency from the predicted level of 20 percent to 11 percent.

In summarizing this section of the paper, we have seen that the predictions of child care costs affecting family decisions such as fertility, participation of the mother in the labor market, AFDC recipiency, and the number of hours worked in the labor market have been upheld in a number of studies. There is general agreement that higher costs of child care lead to lower levels of labor force participation for both married and unmarried women. If the cost of child care included is the cost per child, then the

[12] On the other hand, married women are currently receiving the majority of child care subsidies through the child care tax credit because of the nonrefundability of the tax credit.

number of children also has a negative effect on participation (Blau and Robins, Heckman, Ribar). However, when the entire cost of child care per family is included, the number of young children was shown to have no effect on participation (Connelly 1989a, 1989b, 1990). Though there is agreement on the direction of the effect, there is disagreement among the researchers on the magnitudes of the child care cost effects. Blau and Robins and Ribar argue that the effects are quite substantial, but Connelly's results predict fairly small changes in married women's labor force participation. However, Connelly finds that large declines in the level of AFDC recipiency could be achieved through subsidizing child care costs for unmarried women.

SUMMARY AND CONCLUSIONS

This chapter began by arguing that affordability, accessibility, and quality, as these terms are used in the child care policy debate, are all fundamentally related to the cost of child care. The problem of affordability comes from the large percent of a family's income that is spent on child care. Accessibility, it was argued, is a problem not because of a fundamental flaw in the supply of child care, but because families are unwilling or unable to pay the market cost for the level of quality of child care they demand. Those who find care inaccessible probably demand a very high level of quality. The problem of the predominance of low quality care is also inherently a problem of costs. High quality child care costs more than low quality child care. Parents choose low quality care not out of ignorance but because lower quality care costs less. Thus, accessibility, affordability, and quality are all related to the high cost of quality child care.

Having argued that child care costs are the basis of all three issues, we then sought to answer the question, "What are families actually paying for child care?" and related to that, "What characteristics of the family help us predict how much they will pay?" We found that families differ a great deal in the amount they pay for child care. The majority of families we looked at, families with an employed wife, aged 21 to 55, with at least one child under the age of 13, report no weekly expenditure for child care. The percent paying for child care increased when we limited our sample to those families with at least one child under age 6. We found that families with more children and younger children are more likely to pay for child care and pay more for child care when they pay. The presence of other potential caregivers such as teenagers or other adult family members lowers the probability of paying for care. Location of residence affects the amount paid for care, if one pays. Limiting our sample to those families with one child in, at most, one type of paid care, we found that the probability of paying for child care declined dramatically for older children. Relative care in one's own home is the least likely type of care to involve cash payments, whereas nonrelatives were as likely as group care to be paid. Many child care arrangements with relatives involved in-kind payments, and nonrelative care in the home was the most likely to include both cash and in-kind payments.

After looking at what child care costs are, we then asked the question "What is the effect of differential child care costs on family decision making?" We argued that although extrafamily child care costs can be thought of as affecting the cost of rearing a child, this effect was likely to be small because extrafamily child care substitutes for parental care. Instead, the major impact of the cost of child care should be on the effective wage of the mother in the labor market. Any decision in which the level of the mother's wages is a factor will be affected by changing child care costs. We predicted that increased child care costs would decrease labor force participation of mothers. We also predicted that increased child care costs should lead to fewer hours worked by those mothers who are employed, though this effect was thought to be small because of institutional constraints on the number of hours to be worked and the number of hours per week child care is available. Lastly, we predicted that increased child care costs would lead to an increased rate of AFDC recipiency.

The last section reviewed the economic research that has addressed these issues. Most of the research is quite recent, and this is the first time it has been reviewed together. We found that the evidence supported the predictions listed above. All the studies found a significant negative effect of child care costs on labor market participation of mothers of young children. We also found evidence of a negative effect of child care costs on hours worked in the labor market and a positive effect of child care costs on AFDC recipiency for unmarried women.

The research reviewed offers powerful tools to policymakers for assessing the effect of policy changes on family behavior. The results indicate that the conservative fear that subsidizing child care will push a large number of "stay-at-home moms" into the labor market is unfounded. The labor supply effects of child care costs appear to be small for married women. On the other hand, the results imply that subsidizing the cost of child care could have a substantial impact on AFDC recipiency rates. In addition, the evidence on the determinants of child care costs for unmarried women seems to indicate that unmarried women face a higher average price per unit of child care than do married women, and that unmarried women may compensate for that high price by choosing a lower level of quality. Subsidizing the price of child care for these women would allow them to choose high quality child care for their children. Thus, subsidizing the price of child care for unmarried women is likely to have a positive effect on their children, especially since these children are currently most "at risk" because of low income and family disruption.

Despite the recent flurry of research on the effect of child care costs on a family's decisions, our work as researchers is not yet done. There is still disagreement on the magnitude of the effects. Estimates of child care costs could be improved with more information about other potential caregivers who do not reside with the family. Much work remains to be done on the issue of trade-offs between costs and quality. The results on quality of care chosen by unmarried women were the most tentative of those just discussed because of the difficulty in sorting out price and quality from information about expenditures. To aid in this sorting, we need data that measure the quality of care independently of the level of expenditures and independently of the type of child care used. Measuring the quality of care continues to prove extremely difficult because what constitutes high quality care is difficult to quantify.

Finally, although I believe that the concentration on child care costs has been useful in exposing the inadequacy of the accessibility, affordability, quality trilogy, it was not the intention of this discussion to argue that costs are the only area of concern for child care policy. Another area of concern where public policy can be very useful is the problem of search. Because of the difficulties parents have in assessing child care quality, there are problems in the market bringing providers and demanders together. Information and referral services have been very successful in addressing these problems. Other areas of concern are the location of service delivery, since parents prefer child care very close to home or close to the place of employment, and differences between private costs and benefits of child care versus social costs and benefits of child care. All these are areas that would benefit from further economic analysis.

APPENDIX TABLE A-1

Determinants of Desired Weekly Family Expenditure
on Child Care, Ordinary Least Squares (OLS) Estimation
(uncorrected OLS standard errors in parentheses)

	Married Women		Unmarried Women	
Constant	−133.57	(32.49)	−88.52	(57.24)
Predicted Hours	0.07	(0.20)	0.57	(0.27)
Number of Children				
Aged: 0–2	8.68	(5.66)	19.59	(7.24)
3–5	7.03	(5.95)	17.94	(11.91)
6–12	4.77	(4.61)	8.61	(2.90)
Education	1.40	(0.42)	−0.71	(1.05)
Nonlabor Income[a]	0.88	(3.00)	−0.015	(0.09)
Nonwhite	−5.84	(3.47)	−9.85	(3.69)
Presence of				
Children 13–18	5.52	(10.47)	−1.85	(7.77)
Other adult females	−3.40	(5.72)	14.80	(7.52)
Other adult males	−4.80	10.42	−16.72	(7.11)
Nonemployed females	5.65	(12.19)	−11.25	(11.16)
Nonemployed males	5.32	(7.80)	16.21	(9.49)
SMSA	7.50	(2.08)	7.19	(4.03)
Cost of Living in				
State of Residence				
(Thousands of $)	0.65	(0.17)	0.43	(0.25)
Residence in				
Northeast	−8.82	(3.83)	−5.32	(6.61)
Central	−4.91	(2.50)	−1.54	(4.43)
South	8.94	(3.67)	3.17	(8.77)
lambda[b]	−19.01	(19.43)	1.53	(17.25)
N	567		168	

SOURCE: Table reprinted from Connelly 1989b.

[a]Nonlabor income for married women is total family income minus the mother's own earnings in thousands of dollars; for unmarried women it is monthly property income.
[b]lambda is a selectivity correction term used to correct for the fact that only women who work and pay for care are included in the sample. See Connelly (1989b) for details.

APPENDIX TABLE A-2

Determinants of the Probability of Paying for Child Care Jointly Estimated with the Probability of Being Employed[a] (standard errors in parentheses)

	Married Women		Unmarried Women	
Constant	1.527	(1.247)	.471	(2.614)
Number of Children				
Aged: 0–2	0.463	(0.076)	0.645	(0.203)
3–5	0.501	(0.063)	1.225	(0.175)
6–12	−0.333	(0.055)	−0.041	(0.123)
Presence of				
Children 13–18	−0.727	(0.099)	−0.611	(0.166)
Other adult women	0.087	(0.215)	−0.018	(0.272)
Other adult men	−0.559	(0.221)	0.066	(0.288)
Nonemployed women	0.670	(0.388)	−0.662	(0.300)
Nonemployed men	−0.350	(0.197)	−0.217	(0.342)
Education (in hundreds)	0.955	(1.701)	−2.240	(4.51)
Nonlabor Income	0.201	(0.078)	−0.002	(0.004)
Nonwhite	0.163	(0.113)	−0.132	(0.161)
Cost of Living in State	−0.008	(0.005)	−0.001	(0.011)
SMSA	0.022	(0.086)	0.108	(0.167)
Northeast	0.051	(0.141)	−0.353	(0.279)
Central	0.003	(0.098)	−0.039	(0.218)
South	−0.119	(0.144)	−0.572	(0.327)
rho[b]	−0.463	(0.116)	−0.529	(0.236)

SOURCE: Table reprinted from Connelly 1989b.

[a] Probit coefficient estimates.
[b] rho is the correlation between the unobserved determinants of the probabilities of being employed and paying for child care.

REFERENCES

Blau, David, and Philip Robins. 1988. "Child Care Costs and Family Labor Supply." *The Review of Economics and Statistics* 7:374–381.

———. 1989a. "Fertility, Employment, and Child-Care Costs." *Demography* 26, 2:287–299.

———. 1989b. "Child Care Demand and Labor Supply of Young Mothers over Time." Presented at American Economic Association meetings, December 28. *Demography*, forthcoming, August 1991.

Connelly, Rachel. 1989a. "The Effect of Child Care Costs on Married Women's Labor Force Participation." SIPP Working Paper 8919.

————. 1989b. "Determinants of Weekly Child Care Expenditures: A Comparison of Married and Unmarried Mothers." Working Paper. Brunswick, ME: Bowdoin College.

————. 1990. "The Cost of Child Care and Single Mothers: Its Effect on Labor Force Participation and AFDC Participation." Working Paper. Brunswick, ME: Bowdoin College.

Fuchs, Victor. 1989. "Women's Quest for Economic Equality." *Journal of Economic Perspectives* 3, 1:25–41.

Heckman, James. 1974. "Effects of Child-Care Programs on Women's Work Effort." *Journal of Political Economy* 82:S153–S161.

Hofferth, Sandra. 1989. "What is the Demand for and Supply of Child Care in the U.S.?" Presented for Committee on Education and Labor, U.S. House of Representatives. February 9.

Kisker, Ellen, Rebecca Maynard, Anne Gordon, and Margaret Strain. 1989. "The Child Care Challenge: What Parents Need and What Is Available in Three Metropolitan Areas." Report for Department of Health and Human Services, Assistant Secretary for Planning and Education, Mathematica Policy Research, Princeton, NJ.

Presser, Harriet. 1986. "Shift Work among American Women and Child Care." *Journal of Marriage and the Family* 48:551–563.

Ribar, David. 1990. "Child Care and the Labor Supply of Married Women: Structural Evidence." Unpublished paper. Providence, RI: Brown University.

U.S. Bureau of the Census. 1987. *Who is Minding the Kids? Child Care Arrangements: Winter 1984–85.* Current Population Reports, Series P-70, No. 9. Washington, DC: U.S. Government Printing Office.

Comments on
"The Importance of Child Care Costs to Women's Decision Making"

Sandra L. Hofferth

The objective of these remarks is to put Dr. Connelly's paper in a broader context by addressing four questions: 1. Why does she focus on how much mothers pay for child care? 2. What else is important? 3. What scientific evidence is there on the relationship to child care choice? 4. What remains to be done?

WHY DOES THIS PAPER FOCUS ON HOW MUCH MOTHERS PAY FOR CHILD CARE?

Maternal employment and child care are clearly two important issues for policymakers in the 1990s. Welfare reform emphasizes moving mothers into employment as early as possible. In determining how much it will cost to train, educate, and employ mothers under the Family Support Act, states are concerned about the types of arrangements mothers select and how much they currently pay for such care, as these child care arrangements may have to be subsidized. Newly passed child care legislation will subsidize the child care expenses of some parents. Its costs to taxpayers will depend on what kinds of choices parents make and how much they spend on care. In her chapter, Dr. Connelly focuses on the potential effects of the price of child care that parents face on the choices they make. She uses parents' child care expenditures as a proxy for the price or cost of child care families face.

The Argument of Primacy of Cost

Connelly outlines a clear argument for the primacy of cost in child care decision making. First, cost underlies access to care. To families who cannot afford them, some types of care may be, in effect, unavailable. Second, cost underlies quality as well. A family may wish to purchase high quality care, but cannot afford to, and settles for a lower level of quality. Therefore, cost underlies the entire child care dilemma, so researchers should focus their attention on the price of child care. In her paper, Connelly focuses her attention on one decision that a family makes, the decision for the mother to participate in the labor force. This she sees as a precondition for the payment of child care. She does not discuss the issue of the type of care the family selects, though this is linked with both expenditures and quality. To the extent that a decision about type of child care includes exclusive parental care (which implies that the mother does not work), the two decisions may be one and the same.

Cost Underlies Access to Care: A Critique

There are several reasons to be cautious about focusing solely on the price of care. First, not everyone who is in the labor force or who is employed even uses substitute child care. In some cases, parents share care. In other cases, the mother can care for the child while working. And, as Connelly points out, not everyone pays cash for care. Just because a mother does not pay cash does not mean care has no cost. The cost is what the caregiver gives up because he or she is not doing something else—the opportunity cost. As Blau and Robins showed in their paper (1988), the relative prices of time of the mother and other potential caregivers strongly influence who provides care.

Second, some mothers who are not employed use paid child care for their children. Particularly common today are nursery school programs for 3- to 5-year-olds (Hofferth 1989b). Babysitters are common, as are other forms of care such as lessons, sports, and other activities, particularly for school-age children. Thus having a mother who is not employed does not necessarily imply exclusive parental care. Of course, if child care is used, some of it is used for a very small number of hours. In effect, the mother is still the primary caregiver.

Finally, access to care is also a function of family structure, which affects the number and characteristics of other potential providers available to care for children, such as a husband, older children, or an elderly parent (Hofferth and Wissoker 1990). Unfortunately, this is not something that policymakers can do much about, although they may develop policies that increase the incentives to use a relative rather than a nonrelative as a child care provider.

Cost Underlies Quality: A Critique

Although Connelly (1990) argues that price is a good proxy for quality, there are at present two papers that do not show any evidence for that statement. First, a paper by Waite et al. (1991, forthcoming) using the National Longitudinal Survey of Youth does not find any evidence that parents pay more for arrangements that have lower child–staff ratios, smaller group sizes, or better-trained staff. Now these are based upon parental statements, and the parents may not know what their children are really getting. Second, a paper by Hofferth and Wissoker (1990) finds that the effect of price on the choice of type of child care is not reduced when a control for child–staff ratio is introduced. This too suggests that price does not have a large quality component. If it did, the effect of price would have changed when the quality component was removed. More research is needed, particularly work based upon data on provider fees and characteristics of care, before any conclusions should be drawn, but I would make it an empirical question rather than an assumption.

Finally, I did have some problems with statements about quality drawn from the Survey of Income and Program Participation (SIPP) data, since they contain no direct measure of quality. The educational level of the mother represents so many things that I do not recommend that Connelly suggest it also proxies the quality of child care.

WHAT ELSE IS IMPORTANT?

Although there are many other reasons to be interested in child care, for example, for its effects on children or on the ability of parents to balance work and family responsibilities, here we are concerned with it as an important issue in policy research. Policy research is research that has as its focus a policy issue and that includes as its major exogenous variables policy-manipulatable variables. If it contains only factors that cannot be manipulated, then it has little relevance for policy.

Based upon this criterion, I would agree that price is important and manipulatable, but there are two other important variables that can be affected by policy. These are (1) income and (2) quality of care. Current proposals under consideration in Congress would affect all these three variables in some way. Proposed increases in the Earned Income Tax Credit (EITC) affect incomes, changes in the Child and Dependent Care Tax Credit and set asides through Title XX affect price, and proposed national standards and incentives to improve provider training affect quality.

WHAT EVIDENCE IS THERE FOR THE RELATIONSHIP BETWEEN PRICE, INCOME, QUALITY OF CARE, AND CHILD CARE CHOICE?

There is a growing body of research that has looked at the relationship between each of these policy variables and labor force participation or choice of type of child care arrangement.

Price

Effect on Mothers' Labor Force Participation. A number of studies have shown that the higher the cost of child care, the lower the mother's labor force participation. Blau and Robins (1988, 1989) found the effect of price significant and very large; Connelly (1989, 1990) also found the effect significant but not so large in size.

Effect on Choice. Most previous research has found that the higher the price, the lower the probability of choosing an alternative (Blau and Robins 1988, 1989; Yaeger 1979). In recent research (Hofferth and Wissoker 1990), price was very important in determining parental choice of child care arrangements. The higher the price, the less likely parents were to choose an option. Interestingly, this was most important for sitter care and care by a relative. The effect was large for center care, but not significant in all specifications. More work on fee structures and costs of care is needed. Parents may not be well-enough informed to provide accurate information on costs. In addition, we still do not understand the effects of selection. That is, if those who choose a type of care do so because they can obtain it at a reasonable price, then we would expect that users would face lower prices than those who do not select that type. As a consequence, we may not be accurately representing the prices parents face if we use expenditures as proxies for costs or prices without correcting for this selectivity.

Income

Effect on Maternal Labor Force Participation. Higher earnings of the husband and nonlabor income lower the wife's labor force participation (Hofferth and Wissoker 1990). Higher earnings of the wife raise her own labor force participation (Hofferth and Wissoker 1990).

Effect on Expenditures for Care. According to one study (Hofferth and Wissoker 1990), higher husband's earnings and nonlabor income raise expenditures on center care, but not on sitter care or care by a relative. The same study found that higher wife's earnings do not significantly raise child care expenditures (Hofferth and Wissoker 1990). Connelly (1990) has a measure of nonlabor/husband's income in her expenditure model and does not find that it affects expenditures (though it did in earlier specifications of the model and it continues to affect whether or not they pay [see Connelly 1989]). She does not include a measure of the mother's wages, though she did in earlier work, where she found it to significantly affect expenditures (Connelly 1989). Including the mother's wage is important, since it is an important path through which policies affect behavior.

Effect on Choice of Care. First, husband's earnings/nonlabor income have no effect. Second, greater wives' earnings reduce use of care by the husband, compared with care in a center.

Although they may not affect expenditures, mothers' earnings do affect the extent to which her husband provides substitute care (Hofferth and Wissoker 1990). The more she earns, the less her dependence on her husband. While we found in our study that raising wages would increase reliance on formal modes of care, the effects are much smaller than the effects of reducing the price of care.

What is significant here is that looking at income expands policy options substantially. Though I agree that price is important, one way to improve affordability is to increase family income, or, perhaps even more important, to raise the wages of women. This would do several things: increase their bargaining position in the household (affecting a policy goal not yet mentioned: equity), increase labor force participation, and perhaps increase their ability to select the kind of care that is preferred. The disadvantage, of course, is clear. Since not all this increase will go to child care, the effect on child care use will be small.

Quality of Care

Effect on Labor Force Participation. There is no direct empirical evidence on this question.

Effect on Choice of Care? Research has found that a lower child–staff ratio results in a higher probability of choosing care, but only for care in a day care center (Hofferth and Wissoker 1990). However, the effect is small compared with the effect of price.

Quality is a very important variable for policymakers. There are two issues to be explored here. First is the issue of whether parents are informed about the quality of the care their children are receiving. I think they are. Our research (Hofferth and Wissoker 1990) suggests that parents are informed and that they do take quality into account. In our study we used the ratio of children to staff to obtain a proxy for quality of care. We find that quality is an important dimension of parental choice, though not so strong as price of care. At any given level of price, the higher the quality of care, the more likely it was to be chosen. However, this holds only for day care centers, not for other types of care. This makes some sense. The degree of variation in size is small for family day care. Why should the number of children matter for relative or father care? In fact, the more children, the more likely is the parent to select such care.

The second issue is the size of the effect relative to that of price. In simulations that changed only the price and quality of center care, we found that reducing the price of center care from the predicted average ($2.90/hour) to 0 would triple its use (to 60 percent), whereas reducing the number of children per caregiver from 6:1 to 1:1 would increase its use only by about one-quarter. Reducing the ratio from 12:1 to 6:1 would increase its use by about one-third. Improving quality has important but modest effects on behavior. Thus, this suggests that, although maintaining a high level of quality is an important task, education of parents and continued improvements in affordability may lead to improvements in the quality of care for children. When they can, parents choose quality care.

Parents are also not uninformed when they choose informal care. In much writing, researchers assume that formal care is better or more desirable than informal care. In fact, informal arrangements have lower child–staff ratios but less well-trained staff than formal arrangements. We must be very careful not to suggest that one type of care is better than another. There is no evidence for this; rather, there is substantial quality variation within each type. High quality care, no matter which type, is better for children than low quality care.

WHAT REMAINS TO BE DONE?

In sum, I agree that price is one of the most important factors affecting mothers' decision making regarding their choice of employment and care for their children. However, two other variables—income and quality of the arrangement—need to be explicitly incorporated into the models. Then I feel more confident about our ability to describe decision making in this important area.

There are a number of areas about which we know very little at this point. In particular, we know little about how the quality of the options available affects maternal employment. Maternal employment in this case may be only a proxy for use of nonmaternal care. Therefore, I would recommend doing away with that distinction once we obtain actual data on the child care use by nonemployed mothers and make better use of the information we have on parental care by employed mothers.

What is really needed is a model in which the alternatives are the types of care, ranging from exclusive mother care to part-substitute to a large chunk of substitute time. In all these types, mother care predominates. One of the reasons we have not been able to do this is that we need information about the alternatives available that are not used. In addition, we need information about types of care used by nonemployed mothers. Forming this type of model will not be simple, but will be the next step toward a more realistic model of parental choice of care for children, the bottom line.

Finally, we need to consider carefully for whom the outcomes are of the most interest—parents, children, or caregivers. One policy approach may improve outcomes for one group but not for another. It is not necessarily the case that all interests coincide (see Hofferth 1989a for a discussion of potential conflict between the needs of parents and those of their children). The question indeed, is, can we have it all?

REFERENCES

Blau, David, and P. Robins. 1988. "Child-care Costs and Family Labor Supply." *The Review of Economics and Statistics* 70(August):374–381.

———. 1989. "Fertility, Employment, and Child Care Costs." *Demography* 26(May):287–299.

Connelly, Rachel. 1989. "The Effect of Child Care Costs on Married Women's Labor Force Participation." Unpublished manuscript. Brunswick, ME: Bowdoin College, Department of Economics.

———. 1990. "The Importance of Child Care Costs to Women's Decision-Making." Paper presented at the Carolina Public Policy Conference on "The Economics of Child Care," University of North Carolina at Chapel Hill, May 16.

Hofferth, Sandra. 1989a. "Mothers versus Children: The Real Child Care Debate." Swarthmore, PA: *Swarthmore College Bulletin*, (August).

———. 1989b. "What Is the Demand for and Supply of Child Care in the United States." *Young Children* (July).

Hofferth, Sandra, and D. Wissoker. 1990. "Quality, Price, and Income in Child Care Choice." Paper presented at the annual meeting of the Population Association of America. Toronto, Canada, May.

Waite, L. J., A. Leibowitz, and C. Witsberger. 1991. "What Parents Pay For: Quality of Child Care and Child Care Costs." *Journal of Social Issues.* Vol. 42, No. 2.

Yeager, K. E. 1979. "Cost, Convenience and Quality in Child Care Demand." *Children and Youth Services Review* 1:293–313.

5

Quality, Cost, and Parental Choice of Child Care

Ellen Kisker and Rebecca Maynard

The groundswell of public concern with child care has been fueled by parents, child care providers, and child development experts. Parents claim that the supply of care, especially infant care, is inadequate and the cost is too high. Providers charge that child care worker salaries are too low to attract and retain enough high quality providers. Child development experts are concerned that we are underinvesting in children by not actively promoting the provision of quality and making high quality care accessible to all children, especially those from disadvantaged backgrounds.

Economic models of child care assume that there are predictable relationships between the quality of child care, its cost, and parental choices that would tend to increase supply to meet demand. They assume that parents value higher quality care more than they value lower quality care, that the cost of care is related to quality, that parents are willing to pay higher prices for higher quality care, and that, as the price of care increases, parents will use less care. They also assume that if the demand exceeds supply the price will increase sufficiently to stimulate providers to enter the market. The policy concern is that there are "imperfections" in the child care market that justify substantial public intervention. These concerns are supported by empirical evidence suggesting that much of what may appear to be a market failure may be due to parents, providers, and child development experts viewing child care quality and costs from different perspectives.

This chapter[1] looks at how the quality and cost of care relate to the child care choices being made by parents in an effort to understand better the likely response to various policy options aimed at improving access to and the use of high quality child care. We conclude that parents tend not to be well informed about the full set of child care options potentially available to them. Most often, they make their selections on the basis of quality, convenience, and cost considerations, without examining alternatives. Providers work in an environment in which parents are limited in their ability and willingness to pay for care and in which regulations do not require care to be high quality. The result is that providers often provide care that is below the quality standards of early childhood professionals and for wages that are below their alternative market opportunities. Policies that promote consumer education, increase subsidies, promote effective regulation, and offer incentives to choose high quality care are necessary to make quality care available, affordable, and the "child care of choice."

QUALITY OF CARE

When discussing the quality of child care, two dimensions of quality need to be considered: (1) the characteristics of care that are important to the children, as defined by child care professionals, and (2) the characteristics of care that are important to parents.

Quality of Care for Children

Quality of care has most often been defined by professionals in terms of those characteristics of child care arrangements that lead to positive developmental outcomes for children. The characteristics of care that are indicators of the quality of care include structural features of the care arrangement, such as group size, child–staff ratios, and caregiver training, and process features, such as aspects of caregiver-child interactions, that measure children's daily experiences in care more directly. In summarizing

[1] Paper presented at the Carolina Public Policy Conference on the "Economics of Child Care," Chapel Hill, North Carolina, May 16, 1990.

research on quality of care, the National Academy of Sciences Panel on Child Care Policy (Hayes et al. 1990) described six characteristics of care that have been shown to be associated with child development outcomes:

- Group size, staff–child ratios and caregiver qualifications, all of which affect the level and quality of child-caregiver interactions;

- Caregiver stability and continuity, which has been found to be important for the development of secure attachments and future school adjustment;

- The structure and content of daily activities, which relate to cognitive development; and

- Space and facilities—e.g., the age-appropriateness of the activity areas—which affect social interactions and development.

They conclude that the overall quality of a child care setting is determined by the profile of these dimensions of quality.

Due to limitations of the research showing that these characteristics of care are associated with child development outcomes, the levels of these indicators of quality that constitute acceptable, good quality care have not been well established. Much of the longitudinal research was conducted in the context of high quality programs, such as the Abecedarian Project, the Perry Preschool Project, Head Start programs, and various university day care centers that serve nonrepresentative groups of children, such as at-risk children or children from relatively privileged backgrounds (see, for example, Bryant and Ramey 1987; Berrueta-Clement et al. 1984; McKey et al. 1985; Martin et al. 1990). Complementing this research is research using cross-sectional data sets that has analyzed the relationship between the characteristics of child care arrangements and child outcomes (see, for example, Baydar et al. in press). It is important to recognize that both types of research are limited by the fact that there tend to be strong correlations between the quality of child care settings and the level of psychological and economic stress in the family, which could affect the interpretation of the observed relationships between child care quality and child outcomes. These weaknesses of the research mean that there is no strong empirical basis for suggesting particular thresholds for each of the child care quality indicators.

Although the research is limited, there is an emerging consensus based on the combination of the available research and professional practice on the levels of the quality indicators that define good quality care.[2] The National Academy of Sciences Panel on Child Care Policy (Hayes et al. 1990, p. 99) summarized the consensus defining good quality care in six criteria:

- Minimum staff–child ratios that vary by the age of the child and range from 1:4 for infants to 1:7 for preschoolers;
- Maximum group sizes in centers that range from 6 to 8 for infants to 16 to 20 for preschoolers;
- Requirement of caregiver training that includes child development training;
- Activities that are structured but allow flexibility for child choice;
- Organized and orderly space, with well-differentiated areas for different activities and age groups of children;
- For family day care, a moderate age range of children (e.g., a range of 6 to 24 months).

Quality from the Perspective of Parents

Parents tend to judge the quality of child care by different criteria than do child development experts. Waite et al. (1991) found that parents using better quality care typically did not pay more than other parents, which may indicate that parents do not value the characteristics of quality care as highly as other characteristics of care. Sonenstein (1991) provides evidence that parents may be more concerned about the location, hours, and dependability of child care arrangements than they are about aspects of quality considered important by child development professionals. Parents appear to judge the quality of child care according to (1) whether it offers a safe and healthy environment—many parents express considerable concern about potential child abuse; (2) whether the environment promotes learning—a concern that is especially prevalent for older children (Kisker et al. 1989); and (3) convenience, including location within a 10 to 15 minute radius of home or work and hours that mesh with the mother's work schedule (e.g., accommodating shift work, overtime, and other special needs) (Sonenstein 1991, and Kisker et al. 1989).

---

[2] The emergence of this consensus was influenced by a number of different proposed standards for various programs and settings, including the National Association for the Education of Young Children (NAEYC) accreditation standards, Head Start performance standards, Child Welfare League of America (CWLA) standards, and the Federal Interagency Day Care Regulation (FIDCR) standards.

Parents generally apply these criteria on the basis of very limited knowledge about the qualities of their child care options. Most providers, especially family day care providers, do not advertise their services, and most users do not look at alternative arrangements before placing their child in care (Kisker et al. 1989). The NAS Panel on Child Care Policy concluded that many parents may not be able to weigh considerations of quality in comparison with considerations of cost and convenience, at least partly because looking for out-of-home care is a new and unfamiliar task, the child care delivery system is decentralized, and resource and referral services are not universally available (Hayes et al. 1990).

The Quality of Available Care

There is good and bad quality care in all types of settings—in relative care, family day care, and in centers, as well as in regulated and unregulated settings. The most recently completed national studies of child care providers, the National Day Care Study (NDCS) and the National Day Care Home Study (NDCHS), conducted in the mid-1970s, showed that the quality of care varies substantially across settings. For example, the NDCS showed that fewer than 10 percent of caregivers in center-based child care settings had less than a high school education, compared with 43 percent of family day care providers in the NDCHS (Coelen et al. 1979; Singer et al. 1980). More recent evidence from smaller studies also suggests that child care centers and early education programs are more likely than home-based arrangements to possess characteristics that lead to positive child development outcomes (Kisker et al. 1989; Clarke-Stewart 1987).

Less is known about the variation of quality of care among providers within types of child care arrangements. However, Kisker et al. (1989) found substantial variation in the quality of care provided by providers of the same type. For example, child–staff ratios within age groups in center-based programs ranged from 1:2 to 20:1. Similarly, child–staff ratios in home-based settings ranged from 1:2 to 20:1.

Although all states regulate center care and all but a handful of states have some form of oversight of family day care, the regulations or standards and levels of enforcement vary significantly across states and often do not require good quality care as defined by the professional consensus (Figure 1). For example,

FIGURE 1

Percentage of States With Child Care Regulations Meeting
Professionally Determined Accreditation Standards: 1986

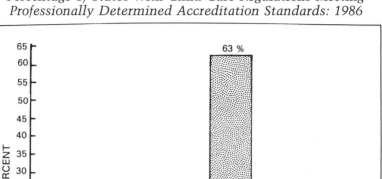

SOURCE: Derived from information in Morgan (1987).

the standards for family day care allow group sizes ranging from six to ten and allow as few as one but as many as four children under age 2 in a setting. Standards for centers include maximum group sizes for 1-year-olds that range from six to twelve children, staff–child ratios for 1-year-olds that range from 1:4 to 1:12, and between one and four inspections a year. Equally important is the fact that the coverage of regulations for family day care varies widely across states (see Figure 2), with the result that more than three-fourths of care is not regulated at all—none of the relative care is regulated, and about 90 percent of nonrelative family day care is unregulated.

THE COST OF CARE

In addition to the quality of care, the affordability of paid child care arrangements is an important dimension of the supply of

FIGURE 2
*Extent of Regulation of Family Day Care
in the United States: 1986*

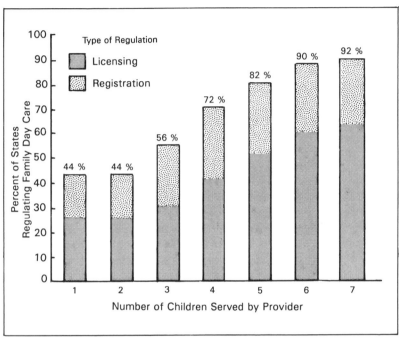

SOURCE: Derived from information in Morgan (1987).

child care. In order for parents to use out-of-home care, it must be available at prices that they can afford. Child care fees often seem quite high to parents who are paying for care, and they consume significant proportions of some families' incomes.

Nationally, parents who pay for their child care arrangements pay an average of between $40 and $60 per week for full-time care (Hofferth 1988). The average price of care varies among different types of care, ranging from $1.15 per hour for relative and family day care to about $1.40 per hour for center-based care. Infant care costs about one-third more than does care for older children (Grubb 1988).

Child care expenditures by parents of preschool children consume a substantial proportion of their income (10 percent of family income and 23 percent of the mother's income), comparable to the proportion of income spent on food (Grubb 1988; Hofferth 1988). Although there is considerable geographic variation in the cost of care, the costs vary relatively little across income groups, with the result that child care consumes a disproportionate share of the income of low-income parents. Poor families spend an average of 32 percent of the mother's income and 22 percent of total family income on child care, despite the fact that they use somewhat less expensive care than do higher-income families (see Figure 3). In addition, single-parent families spend a larger proportion of their incomes on child care than do two-parent families, partly because they have lower incomes and because they have less flexibility to minimize child care costs through shift work (Hofferth 1988; Hayes et al. 1990).

Although child care fees are high from the perspective of parents, they are low from the perspective of child care providers. The average fees paid by parents—approximately $3,500 per year for full-time center-based care and $2,900 per year for full-time family day care—are well below the costs of providing high quality center-based care. Clifford and Russell (1989) estimate that the resource cost of minimally adequate center-based care is $2,900 per child per year, while the cost of high quality center-based care is estimated to be $5,000 per child per year. Similarly, we estimate that the resource cost of minimally adequate family day care is approximately $3,400 per year.[3]

The difference between these resource costs and what parents pay for care of quite good quality is accounted for by four factors. First, providers in both family day care and centers earn low salaries. The National Child Care Staffing Study found that full-time teachers and aides earn an average of less than $10,000 per year (Whitebook et al. 1990), well below the average salary earned by women with similar levels of education in other occupations. Thus, child care teachers are providing hidden subsidies to parents. Second, there are significant uncompensated capital outlays, especially in family day care homes. Third, centers in particular benefit from significant amounts of donated services, space, and equipment. GAO estimates that in high quality center-based programs, in-kind donations account for approximately 12 percent of centers' total resource costs (GAO 1989). Finally, federal and state child care subsidies account for about $6 billion of the total annual outlays for child care (Barnes 1988).

---

[3]If we assume that family day care providers are compensated at the minimum wage, work full-time (50 hours per week), and care for four children, the labor cost alone of providing this care is about $2,700 per child. Allowing the same 25 percent markup for nonlabor costs that we observe in center-based programs, the cost of care rises to $3,400 per child per year.

FIGURE 3
Average Weekly Expenditures on Child Care
as a Percentage of Income

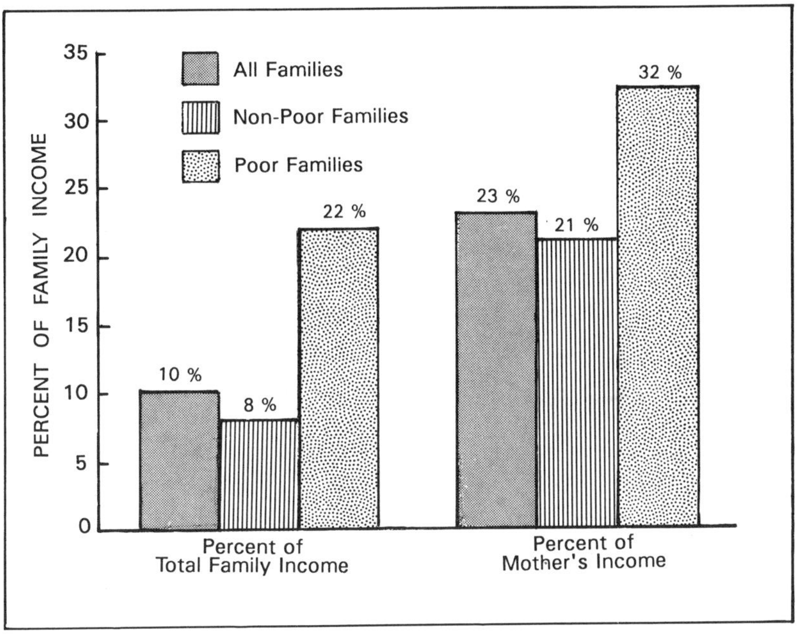

SOURCE: Hofferth (1988).

The Relationship Between Quality and Cost

There is a strong relationship between quality and the resource cost of care, as a result of the fact that quality depends
heavily on the number, quality, and stability of staff providing
care. For example, higher staff–child ratios, more staff training,
and low staff turnover are related to higher quality care, and
higher salaries are associated with the ability to both attract and
retain better-trained staff (Hayes et al. 1990). Although child care
teachers with higher levels of education earn only slightly more
than teachers with lower levels of education, annual turnover
rates are high due to low wages (Whitebook et al. 1990). Therefore, in considering policies that will raise the quality of care
provided, it must be remembered that improving the quality of
care available comes at a price and, for the benefits of improved
care to filter down to children, parents (or someone) must be
willing to pay this price.

Somewhat surprisingly, the price parents pay for child care tends not to be related to the regulatable indicators of child care quality—group size, caregiver/child ratios, physical facilities, and education of the caregiver (Waite et al. 1991). Although quality is the most prevalent reason parents give for their selection of care, the evidence suggests that parents' views of quality are not the same as those of professionals (see the section on "Quality of Care," above). It is also possible that subsidies of particular types and qualities of care play a role in accounting for the low correlation between the quality and price of care.

PARENTAL CHOICE

A critical question in designing child care policies is what factors are important to parents in their selections of providers. Revealed preferences suggest that parents differ in terms of what they look for in selecting their child care providers. Of the 60 percent of mothers of preschool-age children who are in the work force, about one-quarter use center-based care, half use relative care, and another quarter use nonrelative family day care (see Figure 4). A disproportionate share of the center and family day care use is by parents working full time (30 percent of full-time working mothers versus 17 percent of part-time working mothers for centers and 27 percent versus 14 percent for family day care). Relative care is used predominantly by those working part time (59 percent versus 44 percent). A recent survey in three major metropolitan areas found that the majority of parents report being satisfied with their current arrangements (Kisker et al. 1989). Among those who would prefer another arrangement, a majority would prefer to switch from family to center-based care, primarily because they want a more learning-oriented environment.

Parents select their child care arrangements on the basis of quality, location, and cost considerations, in that order. Parents are most likely to report that they selected their child care arrangements, especially for older children, according to the quality of care (Kisker et al. 1989). For many of these parents, high quality child care arrangements are those in which their child will learn more. With respect to location, parents prefer arrangements that are close to home or work. In the three-site study, parents chose child care arrangements that added only an average

FIGURE 4
Type of Child Care Arrangements, by Employment Status

FULL-TIME WORKING MOTHERS   PART-TIME WORKING MOTHERS

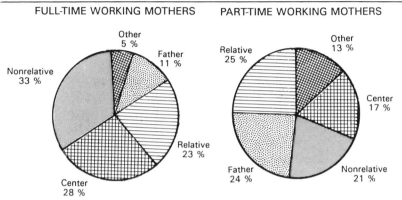

SOURCE: U.S. Department of Commerce (1987, Tables D and 4)

of fifteen minutes to their travel time to work. Finally, evidence
from the three-site study suggests that parents consider weekly
child care costs of $50 to $70, costs that are comparable to average prices paid by parents nationally, as reasonable costs for care.

AREAS OF PUBLIC CONCERN AND POLICY OPTIONS

Parental child care is not a realistic option for many mothers,
particularly poor single mothers. Their need for nonparental
child care gives rise to three major areas of public concern. First,
the *supply of child care is inadequate* to meet the needs of some
families. Although the NAS Panel on Child Care Policy concluded that, in a narrow economic sense, there is no overall
shortage of child care services, they found that several types of
care, including organized infant and toddler programs, before-
and-after school care, programs for handicapped children, comprehensive programs for economically disadvantaged children,
and care during nonstandard hours, are in short supply (Hayes et
al. 1990). In addition, the NAS panel found evidence of a significant shortage of quality child care. Second, the *quality of care
is highly variable,* often inadequate, and often unregulated. Poor
quality care is of particular concern for children from disadvantaged backgrounds who would likely benefit significantly from

an enriched child care experience. Third, the *cost of care* is beyond the means of some families and creates significant hardships for others.

The policy options for addressing these concerns can be broadly categorized as those that are consumer oriented and those that are provider oriented. Consumer-oriented policies address primarily issues of access to care, parental choice, and to a lesser degree, quality of care, while provider-oriented policies emphasize issues of supply and quality of care.

Both the House and the Senate child care bills (HR 3 and S 5) in the recent legislative debate over child care policy contained both consumer-oriented policies *and* a number of provider-oriented policies. The proposed consumer-oriented policies included subsidized slots, vouchers, and tax credits, as well as income supplements in the form of the Earned Income Tax Credit (EITC). The provider-oriented policies included funding for infrastructure improvement through the expansion of Head Start to a full-day program, the development of resource and referral programs, and the development and implementation of regulations.[4] In addition, there have been legislative efforts to implement a parental-leave policy.

Consumer Subsidies

The primary effect of the consumer subsidies included in the recent legislative proposals for child care would be to increase the effective wage of recipients and hence to increase the opportunity cost of parental child care. The lower effective price of nonparental care could have the effect of increasing the quality of care used by parents, but the research showing that the price paid for care is not related to quality suggests that parents may not alter their choice of care in response to the subsidies (Waite et al. 1988). Instead, the main effect is likely to be a change in who is in the work force and using care.

However, consumer subsidies vary in their impact on parental decisions to use child care and in the quality of care selected, depending on the form in which the subsidy is offered. The child care tax credit is the most flexible form of child care subsidy for parents who pay taxes, since the only restriction on the choice of provider is that the individual or program be willing to provide

---

[4] See the chapter by Philip Robins in this volume for a discussion of the provisions of the child care legislation passed by Congress in 1990.

the user with a social security number. Vouchers are the next most flexible form of subsidy, because of their portability among a variety of providers. However, the use of vouchers is generally tied to some form of provider regulation. Although this offers some control over the quality of care that is supported by public funds, it also tends to restrict the options for parents, since many providers are not willing to come under regulations or supervision. Subsidized slots in specific child care settings are the least flexible form of subsidization. While this type of subsidy offers the greatest control over the quality of care that will be used, it is also the most restrictive in terms of parental choice.

Child care subsidies, whether in the form of vouchers, tax credits, or subsidized slots, are income redistribution policies that are likely to have limited real resource costs (unless they alter consumer behavior). Furthermore, because of the small number of users of child care relative to the number of taxpayers, a modest levy on the average taxpayer can make a significant contribution to offsetting the nation's child care costs. For example, under our current child care tax credit policy, each ten dollars of benefits to the average family costs the average taxpayer only one dollar.

Income Subsidies

The earned income tax credit increases the income of low-income families. These income supplements, which are not tied to the use of child care, increase parental options while remaining neutral with respect to both the choice of parental versus nonparental care for two-parent families and the choice of type of provider among child care users. For single-parent families without access to free care, however, they operate more like a child care tax credit, because the only way to take advantage of the credit is to enter the work force and use child care.

Provider Subsidies

Currently about 40 percent of all federal outlays for child care are in the form of direct subsidies to child care providers, mainly Head Start centers and other providers serving low-income children. These types of subsidies allow providers to lower their fees and/or to enhance the quality of care offered. They can also increase the supply of providers by increasing the financial return to child care services. The benefits of the subsidies accrue to both the providers, who may realize higher wages, greater job stability, and an improved work environment, and to the consumers, who benefit from improved quality of care, increased supply of care, and possibly lower costs of care.

Funding for Provider Training and Service Coordination

The funding for training and service coordination that is authorized under both versions of the pending child care legislation should increase the availability of training and hence the supply of trained child care workers. Having more highly trained workers will tend to increase the quality of care offered. However, this increase in the supply of *trained* providers also will tend to increase the wages of child care workers, which could be partly offset by lower staff–child ratios (lower quality of care) to compensate for the wage effect on child care cost. These quality and cost effects could have ripple effects both in labor force participation decisions and in the parents' choices of child care providers.

Service coordination subsidies are expected to increase the supply of care by facilitating entry into the child care market and by enhancing the desirability and profitability of being a child care provider.

Regulations and Standards

Improving child care standards will tend to both improve parents' information about child care quality and reduce the supply of regulated care below that which would otherwise exist due to resource and "hassle" costs associated with compliance. To minimize the tendency of tougher standards and regulations to discourage providers from entering the regulated market and, potentially, encourage some currently regulated providers to go "underground" or out of business, regulations and standards should be tied to other forms of provider and consumer subsidies in order to maintain the current supply of care.

Parental-Leave Policies

The type of parental-leave policy that is currently under serious consideration—unpaid, job-protected leave—will have little impact on the choice of whether to enter the work force or on the selection of child care providers. It is primarily a move to encourage employers to support family policies. If this type of policy were expanded to a paid-leave policy, however, it would have the effect of adding parents (but primarily mothers) to the pool of subsidized child care providers.

CONCLUSION

In a market where parents are not well-informed consumers of child care and providers are not profit-maximizers, policies that promote consumer education, increase subsidies, promote effective regulation, and provide incentives for the provision and use of high quality care are necessary to make quality care available, affordable, and the "child care of choice." The quality of child care is important to children's development, particularly for low-income children whose home environments put them at risk of developmental delays. Because children's development and well-being are critical to society's future well-being, the child care policies that are implemented now will have important long-run implications.

REFERENCES

Barnes, Roberta Ott. 1988. "The Distributional Effects of Alternative Child Care Proposals." Paper presented at the tenth annual meeting of the Association for Public Policy and Management, October.

Baydar, N., R. L. Paikoff, and J. Brooks-Gunn. In press. "Effects of Child-Care Arrangements on Cognitive and Behavioral Outcomes in 3 to 4 Year Olds: Evidence from the Children of the NLSY." *Developmental Psychology.*

Berrueta-Clement, J. R., L. J. Schweinhart, W. S. Barnett, A. S. Epstein, and D. P. Weikart. 1984. *Changed Lives: The Effects of the Perry Preschool Program on Youth Through Age 19.* Ypsilanti, MI: High/Scope Educational Research Foundation.

Besharov, D., and P. Tramontozzi. 1988. *The Costs of Federal Child Care Assistance.* Washington, DC: American Enterprise Institute for Policy Research.

Brush, L. 1988. "Projecting the Costs of Full Day Child Care from the Costs of Head Start." Paper prepared for the Panel on Child Care Policy, Committee on Child Development Research and Public Policy, Commission on Behavioral and Social Sciences and Education, National Research Council, Washington, DC.

Bryant, D. M., and C. T. Ramey. 1987. "An Analysis of the Effectiveness of Early Intervention Programs for High-Risk Children." In *The Effectiveness of Early Intervention for At-Risk and Handicapped Children*, edited by M. Guralnick and C. Bennett, 33–78. New York: Academic Press.

Clarke-Stewart, K. Alison. 1987. "Predicting Child Development from Child Care Forms and Features: The Chicago Study." In *Quality of Child Care: What Does Research Tell Us?* Edited by Deborah A. Phillips. Washington, DC: National Association for the Education of Young Children.

Clifford, R., and S. Russell. 1989. "Financing Programs for Preschool-aged Children." *Theory into Practice.* 28, 1(Winter):19–27.

Coelen, Craig, Frederic Glantz, and Daniel Calore. 1979. *Day Care Centers in the U.S.: A National Profile 1976–77.* Cambridge, MA: Abt Books.

General Accounting Office (GAO). 1989. "Early Childhood Education: Information on Costs and Services at High Quality Centers." GAO/HRD-89-130FS, July.

Grubb, W. N. 1988. "Choices for Children: Policy Options for State Provision of Early Childhood Programs." Unpublished paper. Coral Gables, FL: University of Miami.

Hayes, C., J. Palmer, and M. Zaslow. 1990. *Who Cares for America's Children? Child Care Policy for the 1990s.* Washington, DC: The National Academy of Sciences Press.

Hofferth, Sandra. 1987. "Child Care in the U.S. Statement Before the Select Committee on Children, Youth, and Families." The Urban Institute, Washington, DC.

———. 1988. "The Current Child Care Debate in Context." Unpublished manuscript, Bethesda, MD: National Institute for Child Health and Development, May.

———. 1989. "Child Care Demand and Supply." Hearing on Child Care, Welfare Programs and Tax Credit Proposals. Washington, DC: U.S. Senate Finance Committee.

Kisker, Ellen, Rebecca Maynard, Anne Gordon, and Margaret Strain. 1989. "The Child Care Challenge: What Parents Need and What Is Available in Three Metropolitan Areas." Princeton, NJ: Mathematica Policy Research, Inc., February.

McKey, Ruth Hubbell, Larry Candelli, Harriet Ganson, Barbara Barrett, Catherine McConkey, and Margaret C. Plantz. 1985. "The Impact of Head Start on Children, Families, and Communities." Final report of the Head Start Evaluation Synthesis and Utilization Project. DHHS Publication No. 85-31193, June.

Martin, Sandra L., Craig T. Ramey, and Sharon Ramey. 1990. "The Prevention of Intellectual Impairment in Children of Impoverished Families: Findings of a Randomized Trial of Educational Day Care." *American Journal of Public Health* 80, 7(July).

Morgan, Gwen. 1987. *The National State of Child Care Regulation 1986*. Watertown, MA: Work/Family Directions, Inc.

Singer, Judith D., Steven Fosburg, Barbara Dillon Goodson, and Janet M. Smith. 1980. *National Day Care Home Study: Research Report*. Washington, DC: U.S. Department of Health and Human Services.

Sonnenstein, Freya L. 1991. "The Child Care Preferences of Parents with Young Children: How Little Is Known." In *Parental Leave and Child Care: Setting a Research and Policy Agenda*, edited by Janet Hyde and Marilyn Essex. Philadelphia: Temple University Press.

U.S. Department of Commerce. 1987. *Who's Minding the Kids?* Washington, DC: U.S. Department of Commerce.

Waite, L., A. Leibowitz, and C. Witsberger. 1991. "What Parents Pay for: Child Care Characteristics, Quality and Costs." *Journal of Social Issues* 47, 2.

Whitebook, Marcy, Carollee Howes, and Deborah A. Phillips. 1990. *Who Cares? Child Care Teachers and the Quality of Care in America*. Oakland, CA: Child Care Employee Project.

The Quality of Child Care:
An Economic Perspective

David M. Blau

In the debate over public policy toward child care, the issue of
the quality of care has been one of the most difficult to resolve.
Following a long period of debate and negotiation, in 1990 Congress finally passed legislation that will substantially increase
federal subsidies to child care. One of the main issues of con-
tention in the debate over the new law was whether the new
subsidies would be tied to regulations governing the factors
thought to influence the quality of child care. Proponents of such
tied subsidies argued that there is a clear link documented in the
child development literature between specific features of child
care, such as the child–staff ratio, specialized training in child
development, group size, age-appropriate materials, and children's social, cognitive, and emotional development. Public
funds should be used, it was argued, only to subsidize those
child care providers that comply with regulations intended to
guarantee that the child care environment will foster such development (Whitebook et al. 1990). Federal subsidies through existing programs such as Title XX, Head Start, and the Child Care
Food Program are available only to providers in compliance with
state regulations governing child care quality.

On the other side of the issue are those who argue that tied
subsidies limit the freedom of consumers to choose the type
of child care they consider most appropriate for their children.
Recognizing the validity of the links between the child care environment and child development documented in the literature,
even so, it is argued that parents may have preferences concern-

ing other aspects of child care. These could include convenience, whether the care is by a relative or a neighbor, and whether the care is provided by someone who shares the same religious or other values as the parents. If federal subsidies can be used only for providers designated by government regulations, then, according to this view, consumer choice is unnecessarily restricted. The federal Child Care Tax Credit, which at present accounts for the bulk of all government child care subsidies, imposes few restrictions on the type of provider that can be used.[1] Expansion of the tax credit was supported by those who argue that the government should not limit consumers' freedom of choice in selecting a child care provider. Indeed, some proponents of this view took the argument a step farther and argued that any form of child care subsidy that is tied to labor force participation by the mother unnecessarily restricts the freedom of parents to use the subsidy to enable the mother (or father) to remain home to care for children. Advocates of this view favored an expansion of subsidies, such as tax exemptions for children, which are not restricted to families in which both parents or a single mother work.[2]

The result of the legislative process was a law that provides for expansion of several types of subsidies. These include block grants to states that are designated in part to assist low-income families with child care expenses. In order to be eligible for assistance a family must use a registered or licensed provider that is in compliance with standards set forth in the law, and with any applicable state standards. The law also includes expansion of the Earned Income Tax Credit (EITC), and a new tax credit for children under age one. These tax credits may be used to pay for child care expenses, although they are not restricted to this use, and the type of provider used is not restricted to those meeting regulations. Thus, the new legislation did not resolve the debate over this issue, since it expanded both tied and untied subsidies. The debate is likely to continue, given the very visible place of child care currently in the national agenda.

There are many aspects to the debate over this issue, including

---

[1] The federal Child Care Tax Credit cannot be taken for paid care provided by a relative who is declared as a dependent for tax purposes. The provider must report her social security or employer identification number and have social security taxes withheld. These are the only significant limits on the type of provider that can be used.

[2] See Hayes et al. (1990, pp. 244–248) for a discussion of "child allowance" proposals.

the proper role of the government in the child care market, and the appropriateness of consumer sovereignty in an arena in which the well-being of children is concerned. Economists cannot hope to resolve this debate, but they can contribute to clarifying the issues involved by making the debate a more informed one.

MODELS OF CHILD CARE QUALITY

The child development literature contains many studies that define and measure the quality of child care and the factors that influence it. Some examples include Phillips (1987), Ruopp et al. (1979), Whitebook et al. (1990), and Zigler and Gordon (1982). Hayes et al. (1990) provide an extensive review of this literature. Day care is not a homogeneous service, and it is widely agreed that the experiences and environment faced by children in the preschool years have an important influence on their subsequent development. Parents and society clearly have ample reason to be concerned about the quality of care provided to children. However, child care quality is not an easy concept to make operational. The approach generally taken in the child development literature is to equate the quality of child care with a set of quantifiable features of teacher-child interactions and other aspects of the child care environment that are associated with good scores by children on tests that measure various dimensions of emotional, cognitive, and social development. This approach attempts to make the concept of child care quality as objective as possible by defining it in terms of measurable outcomes that presumably are valued because they are associated either with the happiness of children, or their future success in school, or both.

In contrast, the economic approach to modeling child care quality relies heavily on parents' preferences. Parents may care about the features of the child care environment that lead to good developmental test scores, but they may also care about other features of the child care environment that have little to do with child development as measured by educators, and that in some cases may not be easily measured. If such preferences are common, they could have a significant influence on the decisions made by parents concerning the choice of child care arrangements. A number of studies have attempted to get at this issue directly by asking parents questions about their child care preferences. Other studies attempt to infer parents' preferences by examining the actual choices made by parents in different circumstances, as with different levels of income and in markets with different prices. Both types of studies are reviewed later. Here, however, I elaborate on the differences between the child development and economic approaches to child care quality by describing simple prototype models of each approach and comparing their implications.

Figure 1 presents a schematic representation of what I refer to as the "Educator's Model" of child care quality. Child care quality in this model is defined as child development: a higher quality child care arrangement is one that produces better levels of child development. Child development can be viewed as the output of a "production process" utilizing inputs of teachers' time, materials, and facilities. The productivity of the inputs is determined in part by their attributes, such as the education and training of the caregivers and the age-appropriateness of the materials and facilities, and in part by the type and location of provider, the group size and child–staff ratio, and the child's family background and home situation. The inputs are combined in a production process that can be characterized by the nature of teacher-child, child-child, and child-materials interactions. Examples of specific dimensions of teacher-child interactions thought to be important are shown in Figure 1. This process yields an output that is characterized by a child's performance on one or more child-assessment instruments commonly used in the child development field. The model allows for the child's family background and home situation to have an independent effect on child development outcomes, as well as influencing the production process. It can also allow for interactions between the different groups of inputs.

In order to clarify the terminology, throughout the paper I refer to child care quality as measuring the *output* of child care, that is, child development. I refer to attributes of inputs such as the child–staff ratio and provider training as measures of *input productivity*. It should be recognized that both child care quality and input productivity are multidimensional. This terminology differs from conventional use of the term quality to represent input attributes. I avoid this usage in order to maintain one clearly defined notion of quality. In my terminology, policy can affect input productivity but cannot directly manipulate quality.

This description of the educator's model specifies the "technology" of producing child development, but does not specify

FIGURE 1
An "Educator's Model" of Child Care Quality

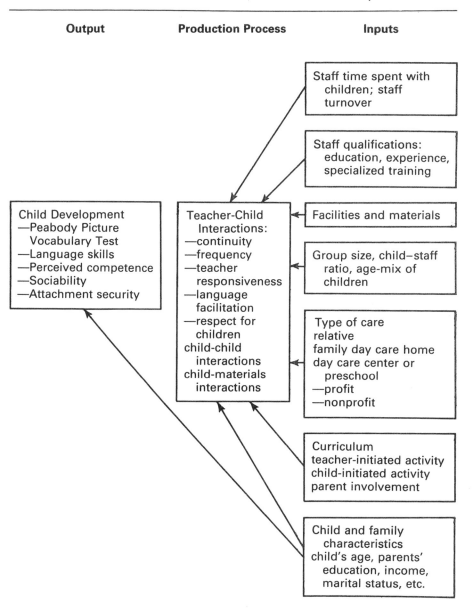

Output   Production Process   Inputs

Staff time spent with children; staff turnover

Staff qualifications: education, experience, specialized training

Child Development
—Peabody Picture Vocabulary Test
—Language skills
—Perceived competence
—Sociability
—Attachment security

Teacher-Child Interactions:
—continuity
—frequency
—teacher responsiveness
—language facilitation
—respect for children
child-child interactions
child-materials interactions

Facilities and materials

Group size, child–staff ratio, age-mix of children

Type of care
relative
family day care home
day care center or preschool
—profit
—nonprofit

Curriculum
teacher-initiated activity
child-initiated activity
parent involvement

Child and family characteristics
child's age, parents' education, income, marital status, etc.

how provider behavior is determined or how parents make decisions on the type of provider to use. It is difficult to find a clear statement of the behavioral assumptions of this model in the literature, but the model is incomplete without some such assumptions. A reasonable assumption that I believe captures the spirit of the child development literature is that child care providers choose input quantities so as to maximize output (child development) per child, subject to given unit input and output prices, and subject to a zero-profit constraint. The idea is that provider behavior is governed by the wish to foster child development while bringing in enough revenue to cover the costs of production.[3] If input and output markets are competitive, then providers will be price-takers, that is, providers will face given input and output prices. I am assuming here for simplicity that child development can be measured by a single continuous unidimensional variable, and that there is an implicit price attached to child development in the market, meaning that parents are willing to pay more for an arrangement that will provide greater child development. I also assume that inputs are continuous and separable. These assumptions are not crucial, but make the analysis conceptually simpler.[4]

This representation of the educator's model of child care quality is admittedly simple, but has some important implications. First, it is relatively straightforward to quantify. The inputs are generally easy to measure, and it is possible to define the productivity of the inputs with meaningful measures of education, training, age-appropriateness of materials, child–staff ratio, type and location of provider, and the like. Second, the educator's model can be used to determine the cost associated with meeting specified regulatory standards. A combination of inputs that on average yields satisfactory performance on child-assessment instruments can be specified, and data on wages, benefits, materials, and facilities costs can be applied to determine the cost of

---

[3]Many day care centers are not-for-profit operations, and Walker (1990a) finds that the majority of family day care homes do not act as profit maximizers. However, there are obviously many for-profit child care providers. It is simple to demonstrate that profit maximizing providers will use less of each input per child than zero-profit output maximizers, but that the relative quantities of inputs chosen will be the same for the two types of providers. This result implies that the responses of the two types of providers to changes in prices and government policy will be similar.

[4]Child care arrangements are in reality bundles of attributes that cannot necessarily be unbundled. That is, certain combinations of attributes may not exist in the market. Accounting for this feature requires a discrete choice model that is more complicated than the continuous choice model described in the text, but it yields similar conclusions.

setting regulatory standards at a given level (Clifford and Russell 1989). Third, the model implies that the quality of child care can be defined independently of parents' preferences. This facilitates the setting of regulatory standards and provides a justification for limiting government subsidies to providers that meet such standards. Such providers can be assumed to be of at least adequate quality, whereas providers that do not meet standards can be assumed to be of inadequate or unknown quality.

There has been a considerable amount of research that attempts to quantify the various relationships specified in the educator's model (see Phillips 1987, and Hayes et al. 1990, for good reviews of this literature). Significant links have often been found between inputs such as the child–staff ratio, group size, and teacher training, and outputs as measured by child-assessment instruments. However, much of this research suffers from the use of small, nonrandom samples of children and child care settings, and from absence of controls for the effects of home and family-background variables. In addition, studies that have compared the outcomes of different types of settings have typically not accounted for the fact that parents may have selected a particular setting in the first place because of certain features of their child's personality or behavior that are related to the outcomes being measured. This could lead to biased results in statistical analysis (Hayes et al. 1990, pp. 58, 66). Nevertheless, the evidence seems consistent enough to justify regarding the links indicated in Figure 1 as useful working hypotheses, if not definitively established facts.

The economic model of child care quality is sketched in Figure 2. The economic model contains the same technology of production of child development as the educator's model. In the economic model, however, parents' preferences play a central role in decision making. Parents are assumed to derive utility from the well-being of their children, as measured by the standard child-assessment instruments, and as produced according to the process described in the educator's model. But parents may also have preferences concerning other aspects of their children's child care arrangement, such as whether the provider is a relative or shares the same religion and values as the parents, and convenience and reliability of the arrangement. Parents also have preferences for goods and services that can be purchased in the market, and for time spent in leisure and other nonwork activities.

According to the economic model, parents choose a child care arrangement, quantities of other goods and services, and nonwork time so as to maximize their utility given their budget constraint. Utility depends on the quantity of each item listed in the column labeled "Parent's Preferences" in Figure 2. The budget constraint incorporates resources such as earnings and other income sources, and the prices of goods and services, including prices of the altenative child care arrangements available. A key assumption of the model is that parents may be willing to substitute among the different items that provide satisfaction in response to changes in the budget constraint. For example, consider two families that have identical preferences (i.e., put the same relative weights on the different items they consume) and the same level of real income, but face different relative prices for child care arrangements. In particular, suppose Family A lives in a community in which the wage rate for a teacher with a degree in early childhood development is higher than in the community where Family B resides. This model predicts that Family A will choose an arrangement with a less well educated provider than Family B. This allows for the possibility that some other input may be changed to at least partially compensate for the lower level of teacher education, such as group size or child–staff ratio. It is possible, of course, that parents' preferences are such that they are in general not willing to make substitutions among inputs and between child well-being as measured by child development assessments and other items from which they derive satisfaction. This is a testable hypothesis, and in the following section I discuss evidence that can help in evaluating it.

In the economic model, substitution possibilities exist at two points. First, as indicated above, it may be possible to substitute among the inputs to the production of child development in response to their relative prices and maintain a given level of child development. This possibility does not seem to have been explored in the child development literature, so its plausibility as a hypothesis is uncertain, but it is an interesting possibility that seems worth investigating empirically. Second, parents might be willing to substitute between child development and convenience and reliability, including substituting care by the mother or a relative for some other form of child care in response to a high cost of high quality market child care or a low wage of the mother.

It is important to note that specifying a model in this manner is not an endorsement of the idea that parents *should* be willing to make such substitutions, but rather an attempt to derive the

FIGURE 2
An Economic Model of Child Care Quality

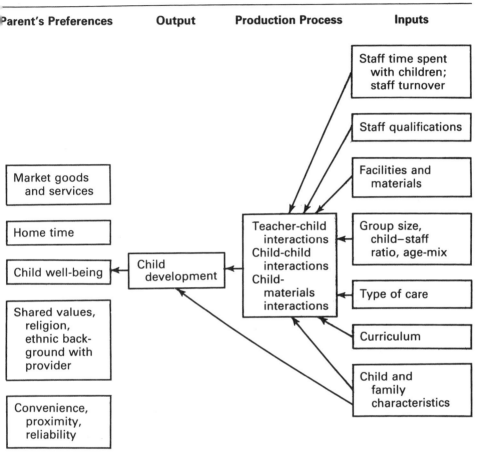

| Parent's Preferences | Output | Production Process | Inputs |

implications for child care policy if parents do in fact behave this way. These implications are discussed later.

The economic model described above has some implications that are potentially testable. First, if children's scores on developmental-assessment instruments are good proxies for those aspects of child well-being that parents care about, then families with higher levels of income should be observed to choose child care arrangements with more productive inputs, other things being equal. Second, unless they are perfectly enforced, regulations may not have the desired effect of increasing the average productivity of inputs to child care. If regulations governing child–staff ratios, group size, and provider training are binding,[5] then they will tend to cause the cost of regulated child care to increase. This could induce some families to use lower-productivity inputs in arrangements that evade the regulations as a substitute for the type of arrangement they would have chosen in the absence of the regulations. This issue is discussed further later on. And third, the relative prices of different types of arrangements should affect the choices made by families concerning child care.

The economic model described here is quite general. The data requirements for estimating it empirically are formidable, and, to date, the model in its full generality has not been estimated. Two recent studies that use simpler versions of this structural model are Michalopolous et al. (1990) and Ribar (1990). Both studies use data from the Survey of Income and Program Participation (SIPP), which lack any measure of input productivity or output quality. As a result, the studies employ some simplifying assumptions concerning child care quality. Michalopolous et al. use reported child care expenditures in the subsample of households that pay for care as a proxy for quality. Ribar treats quality as an unobserved variable determined by observable household characteristics. Neither method of dealing with quality permits the implications of the more general model described here to be tested, but both methods are reasonable simplifications, given current data limitations. As data sets become available that have explicit measures of input productivity and output quality, together with important budget constraint variables, it will be possible to test explicitly implications of the more general model.

---

[5] Here, binding means that the regulation is set at such a level that some providers would have to alter their inputs in order to satisfy the regulation.

EVIDENCE ON QUALITY, COST, AND CHOICE OF MODE

The evidence discussed in this section falls into three categories. First, I review evidence from empirical studies of the demand for child care, the choice of mode, and preferences of parents. Second, evidence from supply studies on the cost-quality relationship is discussed. Finally, I present some new evidence on the determinants of the productivity of the inputs in the child care arrangement chosen by the parents.

Demand and Preference Studies

Several recent studies estimate the effects of the cost of child care on whether a woman chooses to work and on the type of child care chosen.[6] The studies are generally based on large national random samples of families who are surveyed concerning the characteristics of their child care arrangements. These studies consistently indicate that women who face higher child care costs are less likely to work. If they do work, other things being equal, they are more likely to choose an informal or nonmarket type of child care arrangement. This is not a surprising finding, but it is important to note that it indicates that parents are willing to substitute care by the mother or another relative for market care when the price of market care is relatively high, despite the possibility that the quality of the arrangement will be relatively low as measured by child development indicators.

These studies use a variety of data sets and statistical methods, and the findings appear to be robust. However, measuring the price of child care presented some difficult problems in all these studies. The cost of a given type of arrangement is observed only for those families who actually use the method.[7] The users of a given type of child care may not be a representative sample of all families, so considerable care must be taken in estimating what the cost of a given mode of child care would be for families that did not use the mode. Also, the productivity of the child care inputs is likely to affect the cost, and is subject to choice

[6] A partial list of these studies includes Blau and Robins (1988, 1989a, 1990), Connelly (1989, 1990a), Michalopolous et al. (1990), and Ribar (1989, 1990). The pioneering study in this field was Heckman (1974). Connelly reviews several of these studies in detail in her chapter in this volume.

[7] In contrast, studies on the supply of child care have often collected data on fee schedules that do not depend on the particular user.

by families, yielding another potential source of bias. One study that does not suffer from these problems is Robins and Spiegelman (1978). This study used data collected in the Seattle and Denver Income Maintenance Experiments (SIME-DIME) to estimate the impact of the price of child care on the choice between market and nonmarket modes of care among low-income households. Participants in the SIME-DIME were *randomly* assigned (within strata) to treatment and control groups. Those families in the treatment group were eligible for a generous tax-based subsidy for market child care arrangements, while those in the control group were eligible only for the much less generous federal child care deduction.[8] The results showed that treatment families were significantly more likely to use a market arrangement than were the control families. The likelihood of using market care was 14 to 18 percentage points higher for treatment, over control, families. This is an important piece of evidence because it is based on a randomized experiment and therefore does not suffer from the potential measurement and self-selection problems of nonexperimental studies. The nonmarket arrangements in the SIME-DIME study included mainly care by a relative with no direct cost, so the evidence indicates that families are willing to substitute between market care and relative care in response to the cost of market versus relative care.[9]

Another approach to inferring parents' preferences concerning child care is to ask parents direct questions about their preferences. A number of studies have taken this approach recently, analyzing responses to questions about the degree of satisfaction with the current arrangement, the "ideal" arrangement if cost were no object, and the specific characteristics of arrangements that are associated with parents' satisfaction.[10] Many economists have serious reservations about the value of the information gained through answers to such questions. Talk is cheap, and there are no obvious incentives for parents to behave in a manner consistent with their responses to hypothetical questions. Furthermore, there may be some reluctance on the part of parents to admit dissatisfaction with a child care arrangement, since this could be interpreted as a confession of poor parenting perfor-

---

[8] At the time of the SIME-DIME experiments, there was a federal tax deduction for child care expenses, rather than the current tax credit.

[9] Other studies of child care mode choice, such as Lehrer (1989) and Leibowitz et al. (1988), do not estimate the impact of relative prices.

[10] Some recent examples of such studies include Kisker et al. (1989) and Sonenstein and Wolf (1988).

mance. Nevertheless, the information provided in studies of preferences can be useful for what it reveals about the relationship between what parents say is important about child care and their expressed level of satisfaction.

An example that illustrates this well is Sonenstein (1991). She analyzed the preferences of a sample of AFDC mothers with children under the age of three. The mothers rated their most recent child care arrangement on each of fourteen characteristics, and also indicated their overall level of satisfaction with the arrangement. Three-quarters of the sample reported being mostly or completely satisfied with the arrangement, and the other quarter reported being somewhat or not at all satisfied. More importantly, the most significant predictors of satisfaction were the mother's ratings of the convenience of the hours and location of the arrangement and the number of days missed from work as a result of lack of care availability in the arrangement. The child–staff ratio and specialized training of the provider (as reported by the mother) were generally rated by mothers as important attributes of the arrangement, but in fact the mother's ratings of the arrangement on these attributes were not significant predictors of satisfaction. This evidence reveals that, as suggested in the previous section, parents may have preferences over aspects of child care other than those that are indicative of high quality as defined by child development experts.

Supply and Cost Studies

Is it possible to increase the child–staff ratio and at the same time increase the training of the provider to compensate for the higher child–staff ratio and maintain a given level of quality as measured by child-assessment outcomes? If so, this would be an example of input substitutability in the production of quality. Other examples could be suggested easily. The economic model proposed above predicts that if input substitution is possible, then relative input prices should have an impact on the quantities of inputs used. Input-substitution possibilities are a feature of the "technology" of producing child care quality and can in principle be examined by analyzing the relationship between cost, quality, and input prices (the cost function), or by directly analyzing the relationship between the level of quality produced and the amounts and attributes of inputs used (the production function). Unfortunately, no existing studies have provided the analysis needed to determine the extent of input-substitution possibilities in the production of child care quality. This is probably the result of lack of suitable data that combine information on all the relevant variables. In one study in which the relevant data are available (Ruopp et al. 1979, pp. 101–102), the issue is discussed but the statistical power of the analysis to detect input interactions was too limited for any definite conclusions to be drawn. This is an important topic for future research, and the availability of some new data sources in the near future may make such an analysis feasible.[11]

A number of studies have provided descriptive information on the supply side of the child care market. These studies cannot resolve the input substitution issue, but can suggest hypotheses to explore in future work. For example, Walker (1990) provides a multivariate regression analysis of the factors associated with the weekly fees of family day care home providers in three sites. Fees are not the same as costs, but there should be a reasonably close relationship. Walker finds virtually no impact of the provider's education, years of experience in the field, or specialized training on fees. Attributes of the service provided were also generally not associated with the fee. A higher child–staff ratio was associated with lower fees in one site, but higher fees in another site. The main predictors of weekly fees were hours of care, whether the fee covered more than one child (a "package deal") and whether the provider received any direct subsidies. The latter was associated with higher fees.

Mukerjee et al. (1990) analyzed the expenditures reported by a sample of day care centers in Massachusetts. Their regression analysis revealed that expenditures were negatively associated with the child–staff ratio, and that the average education and experience of the staff had a negative effect on expenditure. Prices per unit of labor, capital, and materials were all associated with higher costs. The results of this study cannot be used to infer anything about input substitution because, although the *quantity* of output (hours of care) is controlled for, the *quality* of output (child development assessments) is not. Studies by Hall (1978) and Weiner (1978) using provider surveys from the SIME-DIME study generally found little relationship between costs and input productivity indicators such as the child–staff ratio and provider education and experience in either day care centers

---

[11] The National Child Care Study and the Profiles of Child Care Settings study will provide significantly better national data than those currently available for the analysis of input substitution. See Hofferth (1989) for a description of these studies.

or family day care homes. Whitebook et al. (1990) report that fees paid by parents are positively associated with measures of appropriate caregiving, but there was no multivariate analysis of the relationship between fees or costs and input quality. Ruopp et al. (1979, pp. 111–112) report that the child–staff ratio is an important determinant of costs in day care centers.

This brief survey reveals a surprisingly mixed picture of the association between measures of input attributes and costs. The reasons for this are not clear, but if further analysis reveals only weak associations, then it suggests that using regulations to force providers to improve input productivity could have counterproductive effects (see Walker's chapter in this volume for a good discussion of this issue).

Demand for Input Quality

One issue that has apparently not been directly addressed in the literature is the determinants of the attributes of the provider chosen by parents. There have been several studies of the choice of child care mode, but attributes of child care arrangements can vary substantially within modes. There have also been some studies of the determinants of child care expenditures, but given the mixed evidence on the association between cost or expenditure and input attributes documented above, the determinants of expenditure are not necessarily the same as the determinants of input attributes such as the child–staff ratio and provider training. In this section, I present some descriptive evidence on this issue, derived from the National Longitudinal Survey of Youth (NLSY). These surveys provide information on the characteristics of the child care arrangements used by a sample of young mothers who were employed, in school, or in training at the time of the survey.[12] Table 1 describes the types of child care arrangements used for the youngest child by age of the child for all years in which child care questions were included in the survey (1982–1986). As expected, use of day care centers and preschools increases with age of the child, while use of family day care homes (nonrelative in nonrelative's home) declines with age after age one. The percentage of children cared for by a non-

[12] The NLSY began in 1979 with a representative sample of youths aged 14 to 21, a supplemental sample of black, Hispanic, and disadvantaged white youths, and a military sample. See Blau and Robins (1990) for a detailed description of the child care data available in the surveys.

TABLE 1

*Percent Distribution of Child Care Arrangements,
by Age of the Child, Youngest Child of Women who Are
Employed, in School, or in Training*[a]

Type of Child Care Arrangement	Age of Child						
	0	1	2	3	4	5	6–13[b]
1. Other Parent	18.3	18.7	16.4	14.9	11.0	12.5	12.7
2. Other Relative in Child's Home	16.7	15.9	14.5	15.1	14.7	16.3	13.4
3. Nonrelative in Child's Home	4.2	3.2	3.5	2.9	1.4	2.4	2.5
4. Relative in Relative's Home	25.6	21.6	23.6	19.6	17.4	18.5	20.6
5. Nonrelative in Nonrelative's Home	20.5	24.0	20.2	15.2	12.8	13.0	10.0
6. Day Care Center or Preschool	5.0	9.2	14.5	25.8	34.6	19.6	5.5
7. Mother, at Work	7.6	5.8	6.2	5.8	6.7	7.1	4.5
8. School	0.0	0.0	0.0	0.3	0.2	9.5	25.3
9. Other[c]	2.2	1.6	1.2	0.5	1.1	1.1	5.5
Number of Children	904	1,169	1,062	757	563	368	651

SOURCE: Calculated from the National Longitudinal Survey of Youth.

[a]Because of the longitudinal nature of the survey, many families are included more than once as the child ages.
[b]The arrangement given for school-aged children is the arrangement used when the child is not in school. The arrangement is given as school if the child is in an after-school child care program at school.
[c]Other includes self-care, care by a sibling, and unspecified arrangements.

relative (types 3, 5, and 6 in Table 1) rises from 29.7 percent at age zero to 48.8 percent at age four and then drops to 35 percent at age five and 18 percent at age six as children enter school.

The 1985 and 1986 surveys included questions on the group size, child–staff ratio, training of the provider, and family expenditure on the arrangement. The means of these variables are given by type of arrangement and age of the child in Table 2. The child–staff ratio (as reported by the respondents) averages 1.7 for all forms of relative care, 3.1 for family day care homes, and 6.8 for day care centers and preschools. Training is reported to be rare for all types of care except day care centers and preschools, where it is close to universal. Roughly half the respondents report paying no direct expenditure for a day care center,

TABLE 2

Characteristics of Child Care Arrangements, by Type of
Arrangement and Age of Youngest Child, NLSY: 1985–1986

Type of Child Care Arrangement	Group Size	Child–Staff Ratio	Training	Exp. >0	Weekly Exp.[a]	Exp. per Hour[a]
1. Other Parent	1.9	1.7	—	.06	14.25	.98
2. Other Relative in Child's Home	1.9	1.7	—	.23	27.43	1.46
3. Nonrelative in Child's Home	1.9	1.8	.08	.45	41.12	1.41
4. Relative in Relative's Home	2.0	1.7	—	.33	24.69	.97
5. Nonrelative in Nonrelative's Home	3.5	3.1	.12	.56	33.35	1.30
6. Day Care Center or Preschool	16.2	6.8	.92	.51	33.00	1.42
Age of Child						
0	2.6	2.0	.07	.29	33.59	1.37
1	3.6	2.6	.11	.33	31.20	1.21
2	4.6	2.9	.14	.34	28.95	1.19
3	6.1	3.3	.24	.36	32.20	1.29
4	9.1	4.4	.35	.38	30.71	1.11
5	6.3	3.3	.19	.29	30.45	1.43
6–11	3.8	2.6	.06	.19	22.06	1.73

SOURCE: Calculated from the National Longitudinal Survey of Youth.

[a]Among those with expenditure > 0.

preschool, or family day care home. This may appear surprising, but is a common finding in surveys of child care consumers.[13] Many consumers evidently receive subsidies from state and local programs or directly from the providers. The expenditure information in Table 2 must be interpreted carefully since it does not necessarily reveal the total cost of the service, given the apparent prevalence of subsidies. Reported expenditures are generally highest for care in the child's home, followed by day care centers, preschools, and family day care homes. Expenditures are highest for infants, but do not decline much with age after age one, until school age. The child–staff ratio and provider training rise with age until age four and decline thereafter.

[13] See Blau and Robins (1988, 1989a) for similar evidence on this issue from the Employment Opportunity Pilot Projects, and Connelly (1989) for similar evidence from the Survey of Income and Program Participation.

In Table 3, I present the results of a multiple regression analysis of the determinants of the child–staff ratio and training of the provider chosen for the youngest child by the respondents who use family day care homes and day care centers and preschools. Table 4 gives the means of the variable used in Table 3. This analysis does not account for the fact that families have chosen the type of provider, yielding self-selected samples. If a full range of input attributes exists for both types of providers, then there would not be any self-selection bias, but this cannot be ascertained. The results indicate that, except in the case of the child–staff ratio for family day care, there are few statistically significant predictors. Age of the youngest child and the number of children in the household of various ages are generally the only significant predictors among the household characteristics in the last three columns. Perhaps, surprisingly, regulations do seem to make a difference. A one-unit increase in a state's legal maximum child–staff ratio (CSR) for day care centers (for 2-year-olds) is associated with a .127 increase in the actual average CSR chosen, other things being equal. The effects of CSR regulations for family day care homes are smaller but are also positive and statistically significant. Day care center providers chosen are eight percentage points more likely to have some training if state regulations require training. Given the anecdotal evidence that evasion of regulations is relatively easy, at least among family day care homes (Russell and Clifford 1987) these findings may be viewed as surprising.

There are several significant predictors of the child–staff ratio in family day care homes used by the respondents (column one, Table 3), besides the child's age and number of children in the household. Older mothers (the oldest is 28 in this sample) and more educated mothers choose a higher CSR, but women with higher hourly wage rates choose a lower CSR. The husband's income (and whether a husband is present) has no impact on the input attributes chosen, and the only impact of nonwage income is to reduce the likelihood of choosing a day care center with a trained provider. Thus, there is only very weak evidence that higher income leads families to choose more productive providers, as conventionally measured. The age of the child appears to be the single most important determinant of the attributes of provider chosen.

There is little association between expenditures on child care and input attributes in the NLSY data. The correlation between CSR, training, and expenditure is small and statistically insignificant. In results not reported here, when expenditures are regressed on the same variables used to explain input attributes, the variables associated with more productive attributes are generally not associated with higher expenditure.

Summary

The evidence reviewed above strongly suggests that under some circumstances parents are willing to make trade-offs between the quality of child care as conventionally defined in the child development literature and other features of child care. The evidence on the supply side of the child care market is that the usual measures of input productivity are not significantly associated with family expenditures on child care. There is no evidence available on the degree of substitutability among inputs in the production of quality care. Descriptive evidence from the NLSY suggests that the input attributes chosen by parents are generally unrelated to family income and the mother's education. However, state regulations governing inputs appear to be positively associated with input productivity choice.[14]

POLICY IMPLICATIONS

There are two key policy issues associated with quality, cost, and choice of child care mode: (1) Should regulations governing child care be tightened and made more uniform by extending them to the federal level? (2) Should public subsidies to child care be tied to the use of child care that meets regulations governing input productivity? These questions are part of broader issues concerning the appropriate role of the government in the child care sector, the degree to which the government should subsidize child care, and the ability of parents to make decisions concerning child care that are consistent with society's best interests. I focus the discussion here on the more narrowly defined issues because of the direct relevance of the discussion in the previous sections for those issues.[15]

---

[14] This result could be due to unmeasured state-specific effects associated with both the regulations and the preferences of parents. Blau (1990) presents evidence that such fixed state effects may be important.

[15] See Hayes et al. (1990), Kahn and Kammerman (1987), Robins (1990), and Walker's chapter in this volume for discussion of the broader issues.

TABLE 3

Determinants of Child–Staff Ratio and Provider Training[a]

	Child–Staff Ratio		Provider Training	
	Family Day Care Homes	Day Care Centers and Preschools	Family Day Care Homes	Day Care Centers and Preschools
Intercept	-3.5 (-1.9)*	4.81 (4.43)	-.52 (.33)	1.08 (.36)**
Age of Youngest Child[b]				
One	.41 (.32)	.92 (1.16)	.11 (.05)**	-.06 (.09)
Two	1.12 (.61)*	.58 (1.41)	.26 (.01)**	-.16 (.12)
Three	1.17 (.63)*	1.28 (1.36)	.32 (.10)***	-.13 (.12)
Four	1.51 (.62)***	1.40 (1.45)	.33 (.10)***	-.22 (.13)*
Five	1.34 (.66)**	.98 (1.52)	.17 (.11)	-.11 (.13)
Six +	2.15 (.63)***	5.06 (1.86)***	.20 (.11)*	-.05 (.16)
Mother's Age	.16 (.08)**	-.04 (.17)	.001 (.01)	-.004 (.014)
Mother's Educ.	.18 (.10)*	-.09 (.21)	.028 (.018)	-.001 (.017)
Black	-.62 (.30)**	-.28 (.59)	.01 (.05)	.05 (.05)
Other Race	-.82 (.55)	-1.58 (1.14)	-.10 (.09)	.04 (.08)
Mother's Hourly Wage[c]	-.48 (.26)*	.20 (.53)	-.02 (.04)	.005 (.043)
Husband's Earnings/10000[d]	-.08 (.10)	.04 (.22)	-.023 (.015)	.009 (.023)
Nonwage Income/1000	.15 (.13)	.034 (.070)	-.016 (.021)	-.017 (.006)***
Married	.21 (.30)	-.27 (.61)	.05 (.05)	.03 (.05)

Number of Children in Household aged[e]				
0–1	1.49 (.40)***	1.08 (.82)	.21 (.07)***	−.16 (.09)*
2–3	.85 (.36)**	.46 (.75)	.01 (.06)	−.02 (.07)
4–5	.61 (.26)**	1.20 (.60)**	−.05 (.04)	.02 (.05)
6–8	−.01 (.23)	−.41 (.54)	.04 (.04)	.03 (.04)
9–11	−.42 (.35)	1.11 (.79)	−.07 (.06)	−.10 (.06)
12–14	.97 (.55)*	2.00 (1.11)*	.12 (.10)	.09 (.11)
15–18	−.73 (.46)	−.87 (.69)	−.12 (.07)*	.02 (.06)
Number of Other Adults in Household[f]	.19 (.16)	−.14 (.25)	.03 (.03)	−.01 (.02)
SMSA	.49 (.26)*	.81 (.60)	.06 (.04)	.02 (.05)
Legal Maximum Child–Staff Ratio[g]	.043 (.18)**	.127 (.077)	.0065 (.0029)**	.002 (.006)
State Requires Training[g]	.22 (.22)	.43 (.46)	.048 (.036)	.082 (.037)**
R²[F]	.11 (2.03)	.12 (1.98)	.11 (1.70)	.10 (1.28)
n	451	403	373	320

SOURCE: Calculated from the National Longitudinal Survey of Youth.

[a]The estimates reported are linear regression coefficients and, in parentheses, standard errors.

[b]The omitted category is age zero.

[c]The mother's hourly wage is imputed from a selectivity-corrected regression using all women and all years in the NLSY. See Blau and Robins (1989b) for the wage equation estimates.

[d]Husband's earnings equal zero if no husband is present.

[e]The children are not limited to those of the respondent; they may include her siblings as well as children of other household members.

[f]Other than the respondent and her spouse, if any.

[g]The regulations differ for centers and home-based care. They are taken from Morgan (1987).

* Coefficient estimate is statistically significant at the 10 percent level.

** Coefficient estimate is statistically significant at the 5 percent level.

*** Coefficient estimate is statistically significant at the 1 percent level.

TABLE 4

Sample Means of Variables Used in the Regression Analysis

	Child–Staff Ratio Equation		Provider Training Equation	
	Family Day Care Homes	Day Care Centers and Preschools	Family Day Care Homes	Day Care Centers and Preschools
Child–Staff ratio	3.2	7.0		
Provider Training			.12	.91
Age of Child in Years:				
One	.27	.12	.28	.10
Two	.21	.17	.19	.14
Three	.14	.24	.15	.25
Four	.08	.29	.09	.34
Five	.06	.10	.05	.10
Six +	.07	.03	.06	.03
Mother's Age	24.9	24.9	24.9	24.9
Mother's Educ.	12.3	12.6	12.4	12.6
Black	.23	.44	.24	.46
Other Race	.04	.04	.04	.04
Mother's Wage	4.59	4.63	4.62	4.65
Husband's Earnings/10000	1.1408	.8629	1.1203	.8073
Nonwage Income/1000	.217	.384	.226	.307
Married	.63	.49	.62	.48
Number of Children in the Household Aged:				
0–1	.50	.21	.51	.18
2–3	.42	.47	.43	.44
4–5	.31	.52	.32	.55
6–8	.26	.20	.27	.19
9–11	.10	.07	.10	.07
12–14	.03	.04	.03	.03
15–18	.03	.07	.04	.07
Number of Other Adults in Household	.34	.55	.35	.58
SMSA	.71	.78	.70	
Legal Maximum Child–Staff Ratio	4.8	8.8		
State Requires Training		.49	.47	.51
n	452	403	373	320

SOURCE: Calculated from the National Longitudinal Survey of Youth.

NOTES: The samples described in this table contain observations with no missing data on the dependent and independent variables. There was a large amount of missing data on the child–staff ratio and, particularly, training.

The evidence discussed in the previous section suggests that parents do not necessarily have a strong willingness to pay for conventional indicators of input productivity such as child–staff ratio and provider training. There is solid evidence that parents are willing to substitute among modes of child care in response to relative price changes, and that such substitution will not necessarily enhance the quality of care as measured in the educator's model. Furthermore, there is little evidence that higher productivity providers actually are rewarded for their costly investment in higher productivity. In light of this evidence, what are the likely consequences of imposing tighter regulations governing the child–staff ratio, provider training, and the rest?

If such regulations are enforced, they will raise the cost of providing child care, since meeting the regulations by investing in increased training and hiring more staff is costly. If the higher costs cannot be passed on to consumers, because of consumers' lack of willingness to pay for increased input productivity, then the likely result is that some providers will leave the market, reducing the supply of child care. The providers most likely to close their doors are those of the lowest productivity, as conventionally measured, but the net result is less child care available. If higher costs are passed along to consumers in the form of higher fees, then the likely result is that some parents will substitute away from regulated child care toward cheaper unregulated care that may be of lower productivity than the care purchased in the absence of tighter regulations. In either case, the result is less child care available that meets regulations, and therefore, possibly lower overall output quality. The lower overall quality would result from the fact that detection of home-based providers who do not comply with regulations is quite difficult, so that an "underground" sector can flourish. This is less feasible for day care centers, but if parents are willing to switch from center-based to home-based care, then the effect is the same.[16]

These potentially adverse effects of licensing and regulation in the child care market have been pointed out by others (e.g. Hayes et al. 1990, p. 259).[17] A natural response to these effects

[16]Licensing and regulations are common in other occupations. Hamermesh and Rees (1988, p. 95) review evidence of the effects of licensing in occupations in which evasion of the regulations is difficult, such as law, dentistry, and barbering. The evidence indicates that licensing in these cases restricts supply and raises earnings within the occupation. See also Rottenberg (1980).

[17]Walker's chapter in this volume reviews economic models of perfectly enforced occupational licensure and discusses their implications for the case of child care.

is to provide subsidies to providers or consumers that are tied to the use of child care facilities that comply with regulations. This is the second key policy issue noted above. Advocates of this approach argue that regulations are necessary because parents are poorly informed child care consumers and, left to their own devices, may not choose an arrangement that is optimal for the development of their child (Hayes, et al. 1990, pp. 241–242; Kisker and Maynard in this volume). Parents seek convenience, reliability, low cost, and shared values with the provider, and may be willing to trade quality as conventionally measured for these attributes. But society gains external benefits from children who experience optimal child care programs, and parents do not account for these benefits in their child care decisions. To counteract the negative effects of regulations on supply, it is argued that subsidies can help defray the costs to providers and consumers of complying with tighter regulations.

There are several aspects of this argument that cannot easily be resolved by the sort of economic analysis employed in this chapter. Regulations and licensing requirements limit parents' freedom of choice in arranging child care that they feel is most suitable for themselves and their children. This limitation on free choice is likely to be viewed by some as an unwarranted intrusion by the public sector in family decisions. Others would argue that government already intrudes in many other areas of family decisions, and the benefits to society in terms of child development gained by higher productivity child care outweigh the cost of loss of freedom of choice caused by government standard-setting. A related fundamental question is whether subsidies to child care that are contingent on paid employment by the mother are more appropriate than child allowances that are not limited to families with a mother who enters the labor force. These broad issues cannot be resolved by economic analysis alone because they involve important value judgments and require a specific choice of social goals.

However, economic analysis can shed some light on the narrower question of the likely consequences of tied subsidies and can suggest an alternative policy to accomplish the same goal as tied subsidies. If parents are willing to substitute among child care arrangements with different combinations of attributes, then a subsidy that is tied to the use of arrangements with specific attributes will induce parents to increase their use of arrangements that have more of the subsidized attributes. However, the cost to the government of achieving increased use of high productivity child care could be quite high, or, alternatively, the amount of money the government is willing to spend on tied subsidies may lead to only a modest increase in the demand for high productivity care.[18] This depends crucially on the elasticity of substitution among child care attributes in parents' preferences, that is, the willingness to substitute among attributes in response to relative price changes such as those induced by tied subsidies. The lower the elasticity, the greater is the tied-subsidy-induced relative price change necessary to cause a significant amount of substitution away from unregulated child care that does not meet government standards toward licensed care that complies with regulations.

There is no direct estimate of this elasticity (or elasticities, given multiple attributes) available. The Robins and Spiegelman (1978) study described above probably comes closest to measuring the type of substitution discussed here, since the modes analyzed in that study are defined by whether the care is licensed or not. Their results indicate a substantial price elasticity of demand for licensed care, between 4.0 and 7.0 in absolute value, implying, for example, that a 10 percent reduction in the relative price of licensed care would lead to a 40 to 70 percent increase in the likelihood of using such care, compared to unlicensed or nonmarket (relative) care.[19] However, few families in their study actually used licensed market care (about 10 percent), so even a 70 percent increase would mean only a relatively small change in the proportion using licensed care (from 10 percent to 17 percent). Thus a large percentage change from a low initial base yields only a relatively small absolute change. The important point in this discussion is that substantial increases in tied subsidies may yield only relatively small shifts toward use of licensed care.

An alternative to tied subsidies as a means of promoting increased use of high productivity child care is suggested by this analysis. Parents may be ignorant of the potential benefits to their children of high productivity care.[20] This may lead them

---

[18] A standard result of microeconomic theory is that consumer well-being is increased less by a tied subsidy than by an untied subsidy of the same amount. However, the tied subsidy permits the achievement of social goals where those differ from individual goals. This helps explain the prevalence of tied subsidies, such as food stamps and public housing.

[19] The price and substitution elasticities are not the same thing, but a higher price elasticity implies a higher substitution elasticity, given the definition of the modes used in Robins and Spiegelman.

[20] See the evidence discussed in Hayes et al. (1990, pp. 241–242).

to put a relatively high weight on attributes such as convenience and reliability relative to attributes associated with greater productivity. If this is the case, then directing government subsidies toward efforts to educate parents about child care quality and promote increased availability of information about alternatives could be at least as effective as tied subsidies in increasing the use of high quality care. This is the motivation behind proposals to increase funding of resource and referral agencies and other efforts to improve the availability of information to parents as well as the ability of providers to understand the need for and meet higher standards. The advantage of this approach is that it encourages parents to seek out high quality child care willingly and to serve as monitors of the attributes of inputs and of the production process, a task that is difficult at best for regulatory agencies (Hayes et al. 1990, p. 260; Walker in this volume).

CONCLUSIONS

Educators and economists have different conceptual frameworks for modeling child care quality. Educators stress the process through which children achieve cognitive, emotional, and social development. Economists incorporate this process in their models, but stress the role of parental preferences and substitution in determining the child care choices made by parents. In this chapter I used the predictions of an economic model to derive the likely consequences of two policy proposals: (1) tightening child care standards, and (2) tying increased child care subsidies to the use of licensed and regulated care. In the absence of estimates of some of the important parameters of the model, the consequences discussed in the previous section are somewhat speculative. Nevertheless, the nature of the predictions is such that they should be considered in the ongoing debate over public policy toward child care. The possibilities that tighter regulations could actually result in lower overall quality and that tied subsidies could yield only a relatively small absolute increase in the use of licensed facilities are by no means certain. But they are real possibilities that are not necessarily predicted by the educator's model. As economists continue to estimate empirically the parameters of structural economic models of child care, the likely consequences of these policies will be predictable with greater confidence. If this discussion alerts noneconomists to the possible consequences of such policies, then it will have served its purpose.

This paper was written in connection with the Carolina Public Policy Conference on "The Economics of Child Care" held at the University of North Carolina at Chapel Hill, May 16, 1990. I am grateful to Sarah Mason for typing; to William Prosser, Philip Robins, Sandra Hofferth, and James Walker for helpful comments on a previous draft; and to the Russell Sage Foundation for financial support. I take responsibility for all opinions, errors, and omissions.

REFERENCES

Blau, David M. 1990. "The Labor Supply Effects of Child Care Subsidies." Unpublished manuscript. University of North Carolina at Chapel Hill.

Blau, David M., and Philip K. Robins. 1988. "Child Care Costs and Family Labor Supply." *Review of Economics and Statistics* 70, 3(August):374–381.

———. 1989a. "Fertility, Employment, and Child-Care Costs." *Demography* 26, 2(May):287–299.

———. 1989b. "The Dynamics of Child Care Demand." Institute for Research on Poverty, Discussion Paper no. 898–89. University of Wisconsin, Madison, October. In *Review of Economics and Statistics*, February 1991, under the title "Turnover in Child Care Arrangements."

———. 1990. "Child Care Demand and Labor Supply of Young Mothers over Time." Paper presented at Population Association of America Annual Meeting, Toronto, May. Forthcoming in *Demography*, August, 1991.

Clifford, Richard, and Susan Russell. 1989. "Financing Programs for Preschool-aged Children." *Theory into Practice* 28, 1(Winter): 19–27.

Connelly, Rachel. 1989. "The Effects of Child Care Costs on Married Women's Labor Force Participation." Paper presented at Population Association of America Annual Meeting, Baltimore, March.

———. 1990a. "The Cost of Child Care and Single Mothers: Its Effect on Labor Force Participation and AFDC Participation." Unpublished paper. Brunswick, ME: Bowdoin College.

Hall, Arden. 1978. "Estimating Cost Equations for Day Care." In *Child Care and Public Policy: Studies of the Economic Issues,* edited by P. Robins and S. Weiner. Lexington, MA: Lexington Books.

Hamermesh, Daniel S., and Albert Rees. 1988. *The Economics of Work and Pay.* 4th ed. New York: Harper and Row.

Hayes, Cheryl D., John L. Palmer, and Martha J. Zaslow, eds. 1990. *Who Cares for America's Children: Child Care Policy for the 1990s.* Washington, DC: National Academy Press.

Heckman, James J. 1974. "Effects of Child-Care Programs on Women's Work Effort." *Journal of Political Economy* 82(March/April):136–163.

Hofferth, Sandra. 1989. "National Child Care Survey." Washington, DC: Urban Institute, June.

Kahn, Alfred J., and Sheila B. Kamerman. 1987. *Child Care: Facing the Hard Choices.* Dover, MA: Auburn House.

Kisker, Ellen, Rebecca Maynard, Anne Gordon, and Margaret Strain. 1989. "The Child Care Challenge: What Parents Need and What Is Available in Three Metropolitan Areas." Princeton, NJ: Mathematica Policy Research, Inc.

Lehrer, Evelyn L. 1989. "Preschoolers with Working Mothers: An Analysis of the Determinants of Child Care Arrangements." *Journal of Population Economics* 1:251–268.

Leibowitz, Arleen, Linda J. Waite, and Christina Witsberger. 1988. "Child Care for Preschoolers: Differences by Child's Age." *Demography* 25, 2(May):205–220.

Michalopolous, Charles, Philip K. Robins, and Irwin Garfinkel. 1990. "A Structural Model of Labor Supply and Child Care Demand." Discussion paper. Institute for Research on Poverty, University of Wisconsin, Madison, February.

Morgan, Gwen. 1987. *The National State of Child Care Regulation, 1986.* Watertown, MA: Work/Family Directions, Inc.

Mukerjee, Swati, Sheila Hollowell, and Ann Dryden Witte. 1990. "Provision of Child Care: Cost Functions for Profit-Making and Not-for-Profit Day Care Centers." Unpublished paper. Waltham, MA: Bentley College.

Phillips, Deborah A., ed. 1987. *Quality in Child Care: What Does Research Tell Us?* Washington, DC: National Association for the Education of Young Children.

Ribar, David C. 1989. "Child Care and the Labor Supply of Married Women: Reduced Form Evidence." Unpublished paper. Providence, RI: Brown University, October. Forthcoming in *Journal of Human Resources,* Winter, 1992.

————. 1990. "Child Care and the Labor Supply of Married Women: Structural Evidence." Unpublished paper. Providence, RI: Brown University, May.

Robins, Philip K. 1990. "Federal Financing of Child Care: Alternative Approaches and Economic Implications." *Population Research and Policy Review* 9, 1(January):65–90.

Robins, Philip K., and Robert G. Spiegelman. 1978. "Substitution Among Child Care Modes and the Effect of a Child Care Subsidy Program." In *Child Care and Public Policy: Studies of the Economic Issues,* edited by P. Robins and S. Weiner. Lexington, MA: Lexington Books.

Rottenberg, Simon, ed. 1980. *Regulating the Professions.* Lexington, MA: Lexington Books.

Ruopp, Richard, Jeffrey Travers, Frederic Glantz, and Craig Coelen. 1979. *Children at the Center: Summary Findings and Policy Implications of the National Day Care Study.* Cambridge, MA: Abt Books.

Russell, Susan D., and Richard M. Clifford. 1987. "Child Abuse and Neglect in North Carolina Day Care Programs." *Child Welfare* 66(March-April):149–163.

Sonenstein, Freya L. 1991. "The Child Care Preferences of Parents with Young Children." In *Parental Leave and Child Care: Setting a Research and Policy Agenda,* edited by Janet Hyde and Marilyn Essex. Philadelphia: Temple University Press.

Sonenstein, Freya L., and Douglas A. Wolf. 1988. "Caring for the Children of Welfare Mothers." Paper presented at Population Association of America Annual Meeting, New Orleans.

Walker, James R. 1990. "New Evidence on the Supply of Child Care: A Statistical Portrait of Family Providers and an Analysis of Their Fees." Unpublished paper. University of Wisconsin, Madison. Forthcoming in *Journal of Human Resources* (Winter 1992).

Weiner, Samuel. 1978. "The Child Care Market in Seattle and Denver." In *Child Care and Public Policy: Studies of the Economic Issues,* edited by P. Robins and S. Weiner. Lexington, MA: Lexington Books.

Whitebook, Marcy, Carollee Howes, and Deborah Phillips. 1990. *Who Cares? Child Care Teachers and the Quality of Care in America.* Final report, National Child Care Staffing Study, Child Care Employee Project, Oakland, CA.

Zigler, Edward F., and Edmund W. Gordon, eds. 1982. *Day Care: Scientific and Social Policy Issues.* Boston: Auburn House.

Index

Boldface numbers refer to figures and tables.